POCKET

ENCYCLOPEDIA

ADRIENNE JACK

KINGFISHER BOOKS

For Richard
and my father Carl L. Norris

Kingfisher Books, Grisewood & Dempsey Ltd,
Elsley House, 24–30 Great Titchfield Street,
London W1P 7AD

This revised edition published in 1987 by
Kingfisher Books. First published in 1983.
Reprinted 1984, 1986, 1988

BRITISH LIBRARY CATALOGUING IN PUBLICATION DATA
Jack, Adrienne
    Pocket encyclopedia.—2nd ed.—
    (Kingfisher pocket books)
    1. Children's encyclopedias and
    dictionaries
    I. Title
    032   AG5
ISBN 0-86272-272-1

Editor: Vanessa Clarke
Editorial Assistant: Kate Hayden
Design: John Strange
Cover design: Pinpoint Design Company
Illustrations: Artist Partners Ltd; Jillian
Burgess Artists; Linden Artists; John Martin
and Artists Ltd; Temple Art; George
Thompson; Tudor Art Studio.
Printed in Italy by Vallardi Industrie
Grafiche, Milan.

Introduction

This pocket encyclopedia contains over 500 separate entries. They are arranged in alphabetical order. The information they contain is both interesting and useful.

The encyclopedia can be used in lots of ways. You can look up information on a particular subject for a special project, or you can use it to answer questions that you have been puzzling over, or you can enjoy just browsing through this encyclopedia, stopping when a picture or entry catches your eye.

This is how to look things up:

1. The entries are arranged in *alphabetical order*. Flick through the book until you come to the correct letter for the entry you want to look up. To make this easier, each letter of the alphabet has a different-coloured thumbprint, which is repeated on the side of each page.

2. Use the *cross-reference*. 'See also' followed by a word or words in capital letters appear at the end of many articles. These words are separate alphabetical entries that will give you more information about your subject.

3. Use the *index*. Sometimes the subject you are looking for may not have a main entry. Look up your subject in the index at the end of the book. The information you need may be contained in an entry with a different title. For instance, information on the River Amazon appears in the articles on Brazil and South America.

Aardvark

AARDVARK
The aardvark of Africa is a curious animal. It has no close relatives, although its way of life is like that of the anteater. Aardvarks have strong claws which they use to break open termites' nests.

See also ANTEATER

ABORIGINES
Aborigines are the native people of Australia. They came to Australia thousands of years ago from south-eastern Asia. Aborigines are hunters and food-gatherers. The men hunt emus, kangaroos and game with boomerangs and throwing spears. The women gather nuts, berries, roots and fruits.

But this semi-nomadic way of life has changed for many aborigines. Today many live and

◀ **Different kinds of** African animals gather to drink at a waterhole.

work in the cities or on large farms.

ACIDS
Acids are sour-tasting chemicals. The sour taste of a lemon is caused by *citric* acid. Sour milk contains *lactic* acid. Vinegar contains *acetic* acid. These are weak acids and are harmless. Strong acids, such as *sulphuric* acid, *nitric* acid and *hydrochloric* acid are poisonous.

AFRICA
Africa is the world's second largest continent. Most of the land is a great plateau or tableland, surrounded by a narrow coastal plain. In the east are volcanic mountains such as Mount Kilimanjaro (5895 metres high) and Mount Kenya (5200 metres high).

Some of the longest rivers in the world flow through Africa. They include the Nile (6670 kilometres), the Zaire, once called the Congo (4828 kilometres), and the Niger (4000 kilometres).

The Equator falls near the middle of Africa. The climate near the Equator is hot and wet.

AFRICA

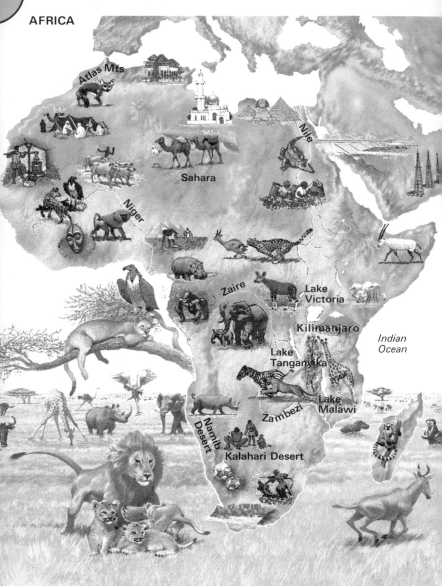

Atlas Mts

Nile

Sahara

Niger

Zaire

Lake Victoria

Kilimanjaro

Indian Ocean

Lake Tanganyika

Lake Malawi

Zambezi

Namib Desert

Kalahari Desert

6

Great rain forests grow here. On either side of the Equator there are vast savannas. These grasslands are dry for most of the year. Travelling away from the savannas you will find areas of scrub, then semi-desert and finally, desert. The Sahara is in the north and the Kalahari is in the south.

A great variety of wild animals live on the high plains of Africa. In game reserves, visitors can see antelopes, elephants, zebras, giraffes, lions and many others.

Much of Africa is thinly populated. In the north the people are mainly Arabs or Berbers. They follow the Muslim religion. South of the Sahara most of the people are Negroes.

Most Africans are farmers, growing crops of maize, yams, sweet potatoes, beans and fruit to feed themselves. Cocoa, coffee, oil palm, tea, tobacco, cotton and sugar are grown to sell to countries all over the world. The country is rich in minerals.

See also COUNTRIES OF THE WORLD; EGYPT; NIGERIA; SOUTH AFRICA.

AIR

Air is the substance that fills the 'empty' space around us. Air is a mixture of gases. Its main gases are nitrogen and oxygen. Oxygen is the gas animals must breathe to live. Air is invisible and has no taste. But when air moves we can feel it as wind. Water vapour, an invisible substance, is also present in air.

A layer of air, the atmosphere, surrounds the Earth. The air in the atmosphere presses down upon us. This is called atmospheric pressure.

See also GAS.

AIRCRAFT

Two American brothers built and flew the first aeroplane in 1903. They were Wilbur and Orville Wright from Dayton, Ohio. Their first flimsy flying machine was made of wood, cloth and wire. It could fly only a few metres and could not travel much faster than a bicycle.

Modern planes are very different from the Wright Brothers' flying machine. They are sleek and streamlined and made of aluminium. With their

Boeing 747 passenger aircraft

7

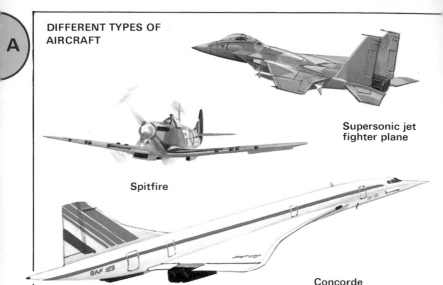

DIFFERENT TYPES OF AIRCRAFT

Supersonic jet fighter plane

Spitfire

Concorde

powerful jet engines they can travel at fantastic speeds.

There are many different types of planes, but, whatever they are like, all planes have certain things in common. They all have wings that enable them to fly. The wings have a special shape, called an *aerofoil*. Its front edge is rounded but it tapers to a point at the rear. All planes have a *tail*. The tail helps to keep the plane travelling on a straight course.

To guide a plane through the air a pilot moves hinged panels, called control surfaces, at the rear of the wings and the tail. Moving these surfaces makes the plane's nose go up or down or to left or right. Many planes are flown with the help of electronics.

Planes are thrust through the air either by a stream, or jet, of gases or by propellers. In a jet engine fuel is burned to make hot gases. As these gases shoot backwards, they cause the plane to shoot forwards. Propellers have a twisted, curved shape and 'screw' themselves through the air when they spin.

See also BLERIOT; JET ENGINE; LINDBERGH; WRIGHT.

ALEXANDER THE GREAT
(356–323 BC)
Alexander was king of Macedonia in Greece and a mighty conqueror. His great dream was to conquer the whole world. He subdued his Greek neighbours in 336 BC. By 327 BC he had

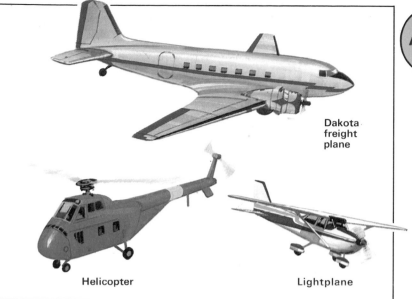

Dakota freight plane

Helicopter

Lightplane

conquered the huge Persian Empire to the east. He then led his men into India, but they were exhausted and he turned back. When he reached Babylon he died of a fever. He was 33.

ALGAE

Algae are the simplest plants. Seaweed is a common algae. Another is the green slime which covers the sides of an aquarium. Algae live where there is moisture.

Like all plants, algae use the energy in sunlight to make their food. In turn, they are food for many water animals, including shellfish and even whales.

There are four kinds of algae. Green algae live near the surface of the water. Lower down live blue-green, brown and red algae.

See also: PLANT SEAWEED.

THREE TYPES OF ALGAE

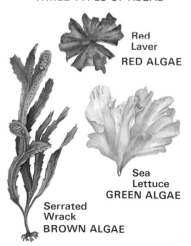

Red Laver
RED ALGAE

Sea Lettuce
GREEN ALGAE

Serrated Wrack
BROWN ALGAE

9

ALLOY

When one metal is mixed with another, the result is an alloy. If copper and zinc are mixed, they form the alloy brass. Copper and tin make the alloy bronze. The most common alloy is steel, which is a mixture of iron and carbon, and often other substances. We use most metals in the form of alloys. They are usually stronger and harder than pure metals.

ALPHABET

An alphabet is a group of letters, or signs, which stand for sounds. It is used to write a language.

The English alphabet comes from the Roman alphabet. It has 26 letters. Many other languages use the same letters, but pronounce them differently. The letters of the Greek alphabet are used as signs by scientists. The first two Greek letters, *alpha* (A) and *beta* (B), give us our word 'alphabet'.

ABCDEFGHIJ

ЗИКЛМНОПРСТУФ

ド・ウオード

ΗΘΙΚΛΜΝΞΟ

ملك طع غ ف خ و ص ض ش ش ن ز ج ج خ ج ث ب أب ي ث ؟

▲ From top to bottom: letters from our alphabet, the Russian, the Japanese phonetic, the Greek and Arabic alphabets.

ALUMINIUM

Aluminium is our most important metal, after iron. It is light, does not rust, and can be made into strong alloys, so is used in the building of aircraft and ships. It conducts heat well and it is often used to make pots and pans. It is also made into thin foil for milk-bottle tops and 'silver' paper.

See also ALLOY; METAL.

▼ An open-cast bauxite mine. Bauxite is an ore from which aluminium is extracted.

AMERICAN INDIAN

When the first European explorers reached America, they thought it was India. So they called the people living there 'Indians'. In fact, the American Indians did come from Asia. Thousands of years ago they crossed the land which then connected Asia with Alaska. Then they moved southwards.

There were many tribes, each with its own customs and way of life. Some Indians lived by hunting and food-gathering. Others were farmers and fishermen.

When the first Europeans came to North America, the Indians were friendly. But later there were quarrels and wars. The Indians were driven from their lands.

▲ **Sitting Bull** led the Sioux Indians against the white settlers. Their greatest victory was at the Battle of Little Big Horn in 1876.

In the 1800s, wagon trains of settlers and gold prospectors crossed the Indian lands. Railways were built and the bison, on which the Indians depended for food, were hunted for meat. The United States Army fought the Indians until the few who were left were forced to go and live in special government reservations.

AMPHIBIAN

Amphibians are cold-blooded animals such as frogs, toads, newts and salamanders. They were the first prehistoric animals to adapt to life on dry land and they still spend part of their lives in water and part on dry land.

All amphibians have backbones and nearly all lay their eggs in water. The young breathe through gills. Later most develop lungs and can leave the water. Amphibians drink by absorbing water through their skins so they must keep themselves moist.

See also FROGS AND TOADS.

AMPHIBIANS

Edible Frog

Smooth Newt

Fire Salamander

11

ANGLO-SAXON

Anglo-Saxons – the Angles, Saxons and Jutes – were people from Germany who settled in Britain in the 5th and 6th centuries. They drove the original Celtic people into Wales and Cornwall. The Anglo-Saxons ruled in Britain until the Norman Conquest in 1066.

ANIMAL

There are two great groups of living things on Earth, animals and plants.

Unlike most plants, most animals can move about. Many have senses with a nervous system and a brain. Senses help their owner to find food and escape enemies. Animals use the oxygen they breathe to burn food, which gives them the energy they need. All animal life developed, or evolved, from simple plant-like creatures. The lowest animals, like the amoeba, consist of one cell. Higher animals are made up of many cells joined together.

The animal kingdom is divided into two groups. The larger is the *invertebrate* group. They include insects, worms, crabs, spiders, snails and starfish.

Animals with backbones are called *vertebrates*. The lowest vertebrates are fishes. Then come amphibians, reptiles, birds and the more advanced mammals. Most mammals give birth to live young. Almost all others lay eggs.

All animals behave in certain ways at certain times. This automatic behaviour such as nest-building, migrating or attacking prey, is called *instinct*. Invertebrates almost always act instinctively. Vertebrates have more complex brains and so they can also learn. Most animals can send each other simple signals through sounds or gestures.

See also BRAIN; CAMOUFLAGE; CELL; EVOLUTION; MIGRATION; PARASITE; REPRODUCTION; SENSES.

Use the Index to find the different animals and animal groups.

INVERTEBRATES

Sea Cucumber (echinoderm)

Butterfly (insect)

12

VERTEBRATES

Eel (fish)

Anaconda (reptile)

Chimpanzee (mammal)

Seal (mammal)

Rhinoceros (mammal)

Flamingo (bird)

A

13

ANT

Ants are called social insects because they live in large colonies. There may be as many as a million ants in one nest.

There are three kinds of ant in a colony – a queen, workers and males. The queen mates with a winged male and spends her whole life laying eggs. The female workers cannot lay eggs. They look after the nest, collect food and care for the young. The males do no work beyond mating with the queen.

There are ants in all parts of the world but the coldest. Some have interesting habits. The umbrella ants chew up leaves and use them for growing food. Legionary or Army ants march in vast columns and eat any living thing in their path.

▼ **A section** through a wood ant's nest, showing different chambers.

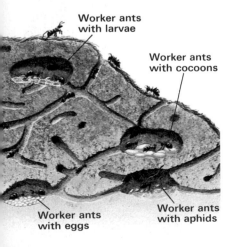

Worker ants with larvae

Worker ants with cocoons

Worker ants with eggs

Worker ants with aphids

ANTARCTIC

The Antarctic continent is covered with a sheet of ice, thousands of metres thick. Its long coastline is a wall of capes and cliffs. There are mountains and volcanoes. The South Pole is near the centre of a high, windswept plain.

The Antarctic is colder than the Arctic. Even in summer, the temperature rarely rises above freezing point. Algae, mosses and lichens are the only plants. There are no land animals, apart from some tiny insects. But the sea is rich in plankton, fish, seals and whales, and there are penguins and other birds.

ANTEATER

The anteater lives in Central and South America. It breaks open the nests of ants and termites with its powerful claws. Then it thrusts its long snout inside and laps up the insects with its sticky tongue.

Another kind of anteater, the pangolin, lives in Africa and Asia. It has scaly armour like an armadillo.

ANTELOPE

The graceful antelopes are related to cattle. They run swiftly on two-hoofed toes and, like cows, chew the cud. Unlike deer, antelopes never shed their horns.

There are antelopes in Africa and Asia. Most live in herds on grassy plains. But some kinds prefer forests or marshes.

▲ **The only people** in Antarctica are scientists. This man is measuring the movement of a glacier.

▶ **Apes** (from top to bottom): gibbon, orang-utan, gorilla, chimpanzee.

APE

Apes are the animals most like human beings. They have the same number of teeth and the same kind of skeleton. They also have the same kind of blood and catch many similar diseases.

After human beings, apes are the most intelligent of all animals. Even so, an ape's brain is only half the size of a person's. Young apes are playful and are easily tamed. Apes use their hands and feet skilfully and can solve simple problems.

Unlike monkeys, apes have no tails. Sometimes they stand erect, but usually they move about on all fours, walking on the knuckles of their hands. the gorilla, chimpanzee, gibbon and orangutan.

ARCHAEOLOGY

Archaeology is the study of how people lived long ago through the clues they left behind – their buildings, weapons, ornaments, coins, bones and tools. Often these clues are buried underground.

Archaeologists excavate, or dig out, buried finds. The deeper they dig, the older the objects they find. From human bones, broken pots, kitchen rubbish and other remains they can learn how the people lived, what foods they ate and what skills they had developed. As a site is excavated, each find is cleaned, labelled and handled with great care for it may be very fragile.

▲ **Archaeologists** mark out the site with a grid to make an accurate plan. Then they carefully remove soil or rubble to uncover the historic remains beneath.

Archaeologists tell the age of an object in several ways. They study the soil and other remains found near it. They can date a find by measuring the amount of natural radioactivity left in certain objects – the carbon-14 method, or by counting the number of tree rings – dendrochronology.

Archaeologists are not only interested in ancient civilizations and buried sites. Industrial archaeology is the study of old factories and machinery.

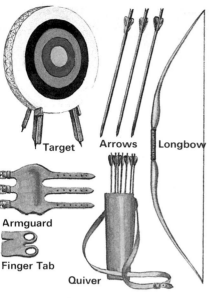

Target Arrows Longbow

Armguard

Finger Tab

Quiver

ARCHERY EQUIPMENT

ARCHERY

The use of bows and arrows is called archery. Prehistoric men used bows for hunting and in battle. In the Middle Ages English archers were famous for their skill with the longbow, which had a longer range than the more complicated crossbow. Bows and arrows became out of date when guns were invented. Today archery is a sport.

ARCHIMEDES (282–212 BC)

Archimedes, a Greek mathematician and philosopher, lived in Sicily. He discovered that if an object is weighed first in air and then in liquid it will lose weight equal to the weight of liquid it displaces.

ARCHITECTURE

Architecture is the art and science of designing buildings. The architect draws the plans which the builders follow. Many different styles of architecture have been used through the ages. Architecture tells the story of how civilizations grow.

The Greeks tried to be perfect in everything they did. Their system of building was quite simple. Rows of tall marble columns supported heavy stone beams, on which the roof was placed.

Greek architecture was later copied by the Romans. But the Roman architects added two important developments: the arch and the vault, a roof supported by arches. The arch was a good way of spanning a wide distance quickly. Small stones and cement could be used instead of heavy marble beams.

In Europe during the Middle Ages stone was the natural building material for building strong castles and long-lasting cathedrals. At first architects followed Roman styles. This is called *Romanesque* architecture. But from around 1150 they began building tall, slender churches and cathedrals. Pointed arches were used instead of round ones. This is called the *Gothic* style.

During the Renaissance architects returned to the Greek and Roman styles. They liked the simple and regular 'classical' designs. But gradually more decoration was added until, by the 1600s, the *Baroque* style was fashionable. It was very ornate. Even straight stone columns were twisted into spiral shapes.

An important development in the 1900s was the introduction of steel and reinforced concrete. These materials allowed architects to build more quickly and very much higher than before. The first very tall buildings, called 'skyscrapers' were built in the United States. Now they are built all over the world.

Today's architects use simple shapes. The architect tries to design a new building so that it will fit in well with other buildings near it.

See also CASTLE; CHURCH; EGYPT, ANCIENT; GREECE, ANCIENT; ROME, ANCIENT.

PERIODS OF ARCHITECTURE

BC	
3200s	Ancient Egyptian begins
600s	Classical Greek begins
100s	Classical Roman begins

AD	
400s	Byzantine period begins
950s	Romanesque period in Northern Europe
1000s	Norman period begins in England
1150s	Gothic period begins in France
1400s	Renaissance period begins in Italy
1600s	Baroque period begins in Italy
1720s	Georgian style begins in England
1750s	Rococo style begins in Italy
1890s	Art Nouveau in Europe
1920s	Modern architecture begins with Functionalism and the International Style

---

ARCTIC

The Arctic is the cold frozen zone around the North Pole. Most of it is frozen sea surrounded by land. At the North Pole the sun never rises in winter. In summer the sun does not set, even at midnight.

During the short Arctic summer, grass, flowers and moss grow on the tundra plains. Arctic animals include seals, walruses, whales, polar bears, foxes, owls, weasels, musk oxen and reindeer. The only people native to the Arctic are the Eskimos. There are many minerals in the Arctic, including coal, oil and iron.

ARGENTINA

Argentina is the second largest country in South America. It is a land of farms and ranches. From them come many different products. Rice, sugar cane and other tropical crops are grown in the north. Cattle and grain come from the central plains, or *pampas*. Grapes and fruit are farmed in the west, and fruit and sheep in the cold, dry south.

Argentina was ruled by Spain from 1516 to 1810. In 1966, military leaders took control of the government. In 1982, Argentina and Britain fought a war over the ownership of the Falkland Islands. See also page 65.

ARCHITECTURE THROUGH THE AGES

Greek Doric: Temple of Neptune, Greece

Roman: Arch of Constantine, Rome, Italy

Byzantine: Sancta Sophia,
Istanbul, Turkey

Renaissance:
Florence Cathedral,
Italy

Gothic: Bourges Cathedral, France

Modern:
◀ Empire State Building,
New York, USA (1920s)
Sydney Opera House,
Australia (1960s)
Sydney, ▶

19

ARMADILLO

This South American mammal looks rather like a small pig, but it is armoured like a tank. It is a timid animal and rolls itself into a ball when frightened. Armadillos eat worms, insects and roots. They dig burrows with their strong claws.

ARMOUR

Before gunpowder was invented, soldiers fought in hand-to-hand combat. To protect their bodies, they wore armour. Leather made good, light armour and could be made stronger by adding plates of bronze or iron. The Greeks and Romans wore helmets, leg armour and breastplates.

Later armourers learned to link together tiny iron rings to produce coats of mail. Mail gave good protection against swords and spears, but steel plate was even stronger. Plate armour covered the whole of a man's body. But even steel armour was no defence against the cannon. By the 1600s soldiers needed to move more quickly, so they began wearing less armour.

ASIA

Asia is the largest continent (44,387,000 square kilometres). It stretches from the Arctic to the Equator and from Japan in the east to the Middle East and Russia in the west. It contains 42 separate countries and its population of 3099 million is over half the world's total population.

ASIA

▲ **Asia has many** differences of climate, wildlife, and ways of life. The main regions are the hot, wet monsoon lands of the south-east, the central high-lying deserts and snow-capped mountains, and the great plains and forests to the north.

20

Arctic Ocean

ral
Mts

USSR

Tibetan
Plateau

Himalayas

INDIA

Indian
Ocean

Gobi
Desert

KOREA

CHINA

Pacific
Ocean

JAPAN

SOUTH-EAST
ASIA

MALAYSIA

INDONESIA

A

21

There are many different types of land and climate in Asia. In the north are evergreen forests, flat grasslands called *steppes*, and cold tundra plains. In central Asia are the world's highest mountains, including the mighty Himalaya mountains. Some of the world's longest rivers flow across the continent.

Almost all Asia's people live either in the fertile river valleys, or on the coastal plains. Most of them are farmers, scraping a living out of a small patch of land. But more and more people are going to live in the cities.

Rice is the chief crop of the warm, wet monsoon lands of southern Asia. Rice and fish are the main foods of many Asians. Other crops are tea, sugar, cotton, coffee and spices.

Asia has many valuable raw materials. The forests provide timber and rubber. There are minerals such as coal, iron, copper and tin. In the Middle East there is oil beneath the desert. The most important industrial country in Asia is Japan, which manufactures many products to sell in other countries. China, Korea and India are rapidly developing.

Asia has a long history of rich and powerful civilizations. The great religions of Christianity, Islam, Hinduism and Buddhism all began in Asia. Asian peoples reached high levels of progress in the arts and sciences long before the rest of the world.

European explorers came to Asia in the 1400s in search of riches and spices. They set up trading stations, and later founded colonies. Today all the countries of Asia are independent and run their own affairs.

See also CHINA; COUNTRIES OF THE WORLD; INDIA; JAPAN; MIDDLE EAST.

ASTRONAUT

An astronaut is a person who travels in space. People have been dreaming of doing this for thousands of years but it was only in April 1961 that the first person in space orbited the Earth. This was the Russian cosmonaut, Yuri Gagarin. A few years later in July 1969 the American, Neil Armstrong, was the first person to set foot on the Moon.

22

Travelling in space is one of the most exciting and dangerous things people have ever done. The astronauts have to be well trained before they can go. For example they must learn to withstand the great force caused by the rocket thrust and to eat, move and sleep without the aid of gravity.

In space there is no air to

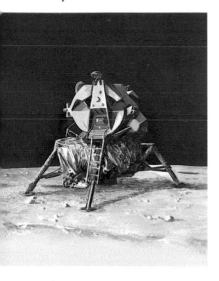

▲ **Astronauts** exploring the Moon. The first astronauts on the Moon were Neil Armstrong and Edwin Aldrin in 1969.

breathe. So astronauts must take air with them in their spacecraft. When they leave their spacecraft, they must put on a spacesuit. This supplies them with air and keeps their bodies at the right temperature.

See also GRAVITY; SPACE FLIGHT.

▲ **Astronomers** in Istanbul in the Middle Ages.

ASTRONOMY

Astronomy is the study of heavenly bodies and their motion. People first began to record what they observed in the heavens in ancient times. They used these records to predict things such as eclipses and comets. Later records of this sort were used to work out, check and correct calendars.

Astronomers now work with a variety of instruments in well-equipped observatories. Their most useful instrument is the telescope, which gathers and strengthens the feeble light from the stars. In recent years astronomers have learned much from information collected by spacecraft on their journeys.

See also COMET; CONSTELLATION; COPERNICUS; GALILEO; METEORS; STAR; TELESCOPE; UNIVERSE.

ATHLETICS

The sport of athletics began with the exercises used to train men for battle. The ancient Greeks loved athletics, and at the Olympic Games young men competed with each other at running, wrestling and throwing.

The modern athlete must train hard to do well. In an athletics match today there are running, or track events; and jumping and throwing, or field events.

ATOM

Every substance is made up of one or more chemical elements. Iron is an element. If you could cut a piece of iron into smaller and smaller pieces, eventually you would be left with tiny particles called atoms. They are the smallest particles of an element that can exist.

At the centre of the atom is a solid *nucleus*. This contains two kinds of particles called *protons* and *neutrons*. The protons have an electric charge. At the outside of the atom are tiny particles called *electrons*, which circle the nucleus. They also have an electric charge, which keeps them attracted to the nucleus.

Every element has a different kind of atom. Atoms of different elements combine to form molecules of a new substance. Two atoms of hydrogen (H) combine with one atom of oxygen (O) to form one molecule of water. We can therefore represent water like this: H_2O.

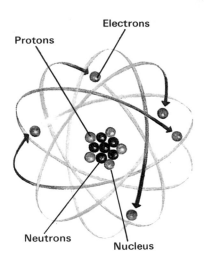

▲ **An atom** of boron. The nucleus, made up of protons and neutrons, is surrounded by whizzing electrons.

AUSTRALIA

Australia is the largest island in the world and the smallest continent. Low mountains run all the way down the east coast. Most of the centre is grassy plain and the western part consists of flat scrub-land, barren, rolling hills and desert. About four-fifths of the continent is hot desert.

Along the north-eastern coast is a chain of beautifully coloured coral reefs, islands and sand-banks called the Great Barrier Reef. Most people have settled in the south-east where there is enough water.

The seasons are the exact opposite of those in the northern hemisphere. When it is spring in

Britain it is autumn in Australia. Winters are mild and there is plenty of sunshine.

Although the Dutch discovered Australia in 1606 they did not settle it. Captain Cook claimed eastern Australia for Britain in 1770. In 1788, 800 convicts were landed in Botany Bay. These convicts became Australia's earliest colonists.

Australia is a farming country. It produces wool, dairy foods, meat, fruit and wheat to sell to the rest of the world. Australia mines valuable minerals, too. They include gold, silver, coal, lead, copper, tin and uranium.

It is also the home of many strange plants and animals, such as the platypus and emu, which are found nowhere else in the world. Many of the native animals are marsupials, or animals that carry their young around in pouches until they are old enough to look after themselves. These include the kangaroo, koala and wombat.

See also EMU; KANGAROO; KOALA; MARSUPIAL; PLATYPUS and page 65.

▼ **Australia** is a huge island. Most of the centre is hot and dry. All the fertile, well-watered lands are near the coasts. Australia's plants and animals are unlike any others in the world.

AUSTRALIA

Coral Sea
Great Barrier Reef
Timor Sea
Great Sandy Desert
Ayer's Rock
Great Dividing Range
Gibson Desert
Great Victoria Desert
Nullarbor Plain
Indian Ocean
Tasmania

AUSTRIA

The independent republic of Austria is a land of tall mountains, thick forest, quiet meadowland and farms, and beautiful lakes. The forests are Austria's greatest wealth. They provide timber for the saw mills, factories and for export. Iron ore, lead, zinc and copper are mined and steel and paper are manufactured. See also page 64.

AZTEC

The Aztecs were an ancient people who lived in Mexico. Their great city, Tenochtitlán, had huge temple pyramids. The city was built on a lake, so people travelled about in boats. When the Spanish explorer Cortes entered Mexico in 1519, he was astonished to find such a civilization.

The Spaniards wanted the Aztecs' gold. Although their army was small, they had guns and horses, and were able to conquer the Aztecs.

▲ The ruins of an Aztec pyramid.

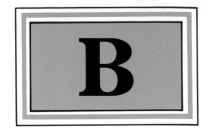

BACH, Johann Sebastian
(1685–1750)

J. S. Bach is the most famous of a great family of German composers and musicians. He was master of the organ and composed hundreds of pieces of music, including many choral works.

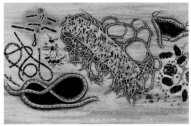

▲ **Some bacteria** have tiny hairs to help them move about.

BACTERIA

Bacteria are among the smallest living things. Each one is made up of just a single cell, and can be seen only under a microscope. There are millions of bacteria all around us.

Some bacteria feed on dead creatures and waste, causing them to decay. They make the soil rich and help plants grow. Bacteria also turn meat rotten and milk sour. Some bacteria cause disease.

Badger

BADGER

The badger is a relative of the weasel. It is a powerfully built animal with short legs and a black and white striped head.

Badgers dig deep burrows called sets, from which they emerge after dark to find food. They will fight fiercely if attacked but, left alone, are peaceful animals.

BALLET

Ballet is a classic form of dance performed on the stage. It may tell a story or act out an idea or feeling. Classical ballet is based on a number of set positions and movements which are arranged by a choreographer in various ways. Ballet was first recognized in France where the Royal Academy of Dancing was founded in 1661. Modern ballet allows dancers more freedom of movement.

Ballet is recorded in a special way and can be danced over and over again. Some of the ballets performed today were first presented 140 years ago.

BALLOONS AND AIRSHIPS

B

Balloons and airships use gases such as helium, hydrogen and hot air to fly. These gases are lighter than air. While balloons can only drift in the wind, airships can be flown.

The first balloon to carry people was built by the Montgolfier brothers in 1783. A fire was built beneath an open-ended bag filling it with hot air.

Today balloons are used mostly by weathermen. Those called radiosondes carry instruments into the air to measure such things as temperature and atmospheric pressure. Balloons are also used for sport.

Airships are usually bigger than balloons and are cigar-shaped. They have enclosed cabins and engines.

▼ Galina and Valery Panov dance in a scene from Wolf Trap.

27

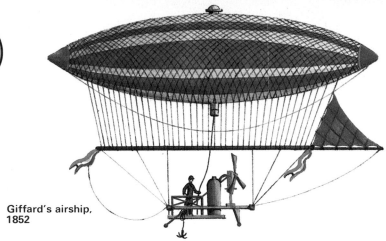

Giffard's airship, 1852

The first airship flew in 1852. They came to be used for travel and in war. But they proved to be unsafe and so were not built for these purposes after the 1930s. Airships are used today for advertising and for moving heavy, awkwardly placed goods.

BAROMETER

A barometer is an instrument used to measure air pressure. It can help forecast the weather and measure height above sea-level.

There are two major types of barometer: the mercury and the aneroid. The aneroid barometer is the more commonly used. It consists of a drum from which most of the air has been removed. When the pressure of the air outside the drum changes, the size of the drum changes. This change in size is recorded by a pointer on a scale.

Generally speaking, if a barometer shows high pressure, it means good weather.

BASKETBALL

Basketball is played on a court by two teams of five players each. Points are made by throwing a ball through a basket. Each 'basket' counts as two points. Free throws, for fouls, count as one. It helps to be tall in this game.

BAT

Bats are the only mammals which can fly. Their wings are covered with thin skin. They sleep by day, hanging upside down in caves or other dark places.

Insect-eating bats cannot see well. Yet they can fly in the dark without bumping into obstacles. They send out very high-pitched squeaks and listen for the echo which bounces off the things around them.

The vampire bat of South America feeds on the blood of other animals. The largest bats are fruit-eaters.

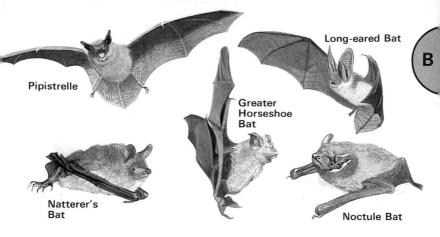

Pipistrelle

Long-eared Bat

B

Greater
Horseshoe
Bat

Natterer's
Bat

Noctule Bat

BEAR

Although bears may look cuddly and playful, they are dangerous animals. They are very strong and have sharp claws. Although some bears can be tamed, they may still attack without warning.

Bears live mainly in forests and mountains. They are meat-eating mammals. But they will also eat almost any kind of plant or insect. Some bears hibernate (sleep) during the winter, living on fat stored in their bodies.

There are several different kinds of bears. The largest – the grizzly, the Kodiak and the polar – are from North America. The polar bear also lives in northern Europe. The sun bear, from Asia, is the smallest.

▼ **A polar bear** waits by a hole in the ice, hoping to catch a seal.

BEAVER

These rodents have stout bodies and short legs. Their webbed feet and paddle-like tails make them good swimmers. They can stay under water for several minutes.

Beavers live in family groups. They make a home safe from enemies by damming streams and small rivers with branches, stones and mud. In the pool formed behind the dam, the beavers build their lodge, a dome-shaped den of mud and sticks with an underwater entrance.

BEE

Bees are very useful insects. They make honey and wax. More importantly, bees help to make seeds by pollinating plants.

Some bees are solitary. Others, such as the bumblebee and the

30

▲ **A beavers' lodge.** The beavers go in and out underwater but sleep in a dry chamber inside.

honeybee are social insects and live in large colonies.

Social insects build a nest or hive. In every hive there are many worker bees, a few male drones and a queen.

After mating with a drone, the queen bee begins to lay thousands of eggs. The workers are small female bees. They build the wax cells of the comb and gather nectar and pollen from flowers to store inside. Workers also feed the queen and the larvae and guard the hive. Drones do no work and in the autumn they are driven from the hive to die.

See also INSECT.

BEETHOVEN, Ludwig van
(1770–1827)

Beethoven was a German composer who wrote some of the world's greatest music. He began writing music while a boy. In later life he went deaf, but still continued to write music.

See also MUSIC.

BEETLE

Beetles are one of the largest groups of insects. Beetles have two pairs of wings, but only the back pair are used for flying. The front pair have become hard wing covers.

Beetles and their larvae can be harmful. The Colorado beetle attacks potato crops. Grain weevils damage corn. Woodworms, larvae of the furniture beetle, bore tunnels in timber.

Other beetles are useful. Ladybirds eat greenfly and burying beetles clear dead animals away.

See also INSECT.

◀ **A queen bee** circled by workers. She lays eggs in wax cells.

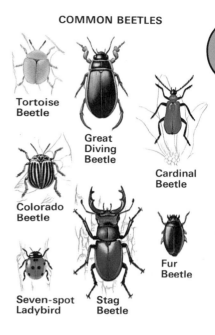

COMMON BEETLES

B

Tortoise Beetle

Great Diving Beetle

Cardinal Beetle

Colorado Beetle

Fur Beetle

Seven-spot Ladybird

Stag Beetle

BELGIUM

Belgium is a small country wedged between France, Germany, Luxembourg and the Netherlands. Its population of 9,941,000 makes it one of the most densely populated countries in Europe. It has many industries and great quantities of coal. Belgium has three languages – Flemish, French and German. Its capital, Brussels, is the headquarters for the EEC. See also page 64.

BIBLE

The Bible is in two parts – the Old and New Testaments. It was written at different times and by different people, but most of it is thousands of years old.

The Old Testament is held sacred by Jews and Christians. It tells the stories of the Jewish people, their kings and prophets. The New Testament is sacred only to Christians. It contains the four gospels of Matthew, Mark, Luke and John. Gospel means 'good news'. Each of these 'evangelists" tells the stories of Jesus' life: his birth in Bethlehem, his teaching, his death on the cross and his resurrection.

See also JESUS CHRIST; CHRISTIANITY.

BIRD

All birds have wings, though some cannot fly. They have feathers, and beaks instead of jaws.

Most birds are perfectly built for flying. Their bones are hollow, light but strong. Their wing muscles are powerful. Their feathers help them fly, and also keep them warm and dry.

◀ **A penny farthing** from the 1880s.
▼ **A racing bicycle** used today.

BICYCLE

The first bicycle was built in about 1790 by a Frenchman named De Sivrac. Early bicycles were steered by the front wheel and propelled by the rider pushing his feet on the ground. Later bicycles had pedals to propel them. The famous penny farthing bicycle had the pedals attached to its huge front wheel. More and more improvements were made until, by the end of the 1800s, bicycles resembled today's models.

The modern bicycle is propelled by pedals attached to cranks. The cranks turn a toothed chain which is attached to a cog on the rear wheel.

Flying is hard work and birds use up a lot of energy, so they spend a lot of time eating. Birds rely mostly on eyesight to find food, but their taste and hearing are also good. Their sense of smell is poor. Birds are born with all the skills they will need. Much of their behaviour is not learned but comes from instinct.

Birds reproduce by laying eggs. In order to hatch, the eggs must be kept warm, so parent birds sit on them. When the young hatch, they are helpless and must be fed.

See also CUCKOO; DUCKS AND GEESE; EAGLE; EMU; HUMMINGBIRD; KIWI; OSTRICH; OWL; PARROT; PENGUIN; SWAN.

Toucan

Hummingbird

Crowned cranes

Spoonbill

Bluejay

Bird of
Paradise

Crossbill

Blackbird

Pheasant

▲ **Birds** from different
parts of the world. Their
beaks are different
shapes to suit the kind
of food they eat.

33

BISON

Bison are wild cattle. They are large, powerful animals with humped shoulders, thick fur and short horns.

The North American bison is sometimes called the buffalo. Vast herds of bison provided food for the American Indians. But white men killed so many that the bison nearly died out. Now it is a protected animal. The European bison, or wisent, is also rare.

BLACK HOLE

When a star begins to lose its ability to produce energy it begins a slow process of collapsing onto itself. The atoms which make up the star get closer and closer together and the star forms a ball about as big as the Earth. This star is called a *white dwarf*.

▼ **Bison on** the North American prairies.

If the collapsing star is very big or explodes powerfully, its atoms may become even more densely packed. The electrons and protons combine to become neutrons. This is called a *neutron star*.

When even the neutrons are crushed by gravity, the entire star disappears into a *black hole*. It is called a black hole because the pull of gravity is so great that not even light can escape from it.

See also STAR.

BLERIOT, Louis (1872–1936)

Blériot, a Frenchman, was one of the great pilots in the history of flying. He designed and built many of the early aeroplanes. In 1909 the *Daily Mail* newspaper offered a prize to the first person to fly the English Channel. Blériot accepted this challenge and flew the 40 kilometres from Calais to Dover in 37 minutes. He continued to design and later to manufacture aeroplanes.

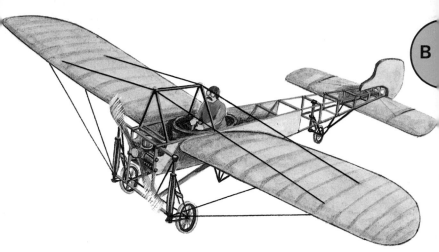

BLOOD

Blood is made up of red and white cells that float in a liquid called plasma. It is pumped round the body by the heart. There are about five litres in an average adult.

Blood serves several very important functions. Its main purpose is to carry substances round the body. It takes oxygen from the lungs and nutrients from the intestines and distributes them to body cells. It takes waste products from the cells to the lungs and kidneys. Blood also carries heat around the body from the muscles where most of it is produced.

Finally, blood protects the body. It is able to clot when the skin is wounded and it fights infection. The white cells can attack germs and can produce substances to counteract poisons produced by the germs.

See also HEART.

▲ **Louis Blériot** in his monoplane.

▼ **The network of arteries** which circulate the blood around the body.

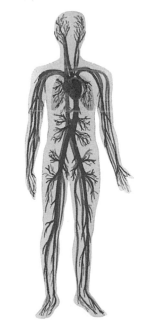

BOADICEA (died AD 62)

Boadicea was queen of the Iceni tribe during the Roman occupation of Britain. When the Romans seized Iceni property and ill-treated them, Boadicea and the Iceni rebelled. Many Britons joined them. When they were ·finally defeated, Boadicea poisoned herself.

BONE

Bones make up the framework or skeleton of all vertebrates (animals with backbones). They are very strong. Two-thirds of a bone is mineral which makes it hard. One third is animal matter which makes it difficult to break.

Bones have several functions. They protect important organs such as the brain, heart and lungs, and support the limbs. Some bones are hollow and filled with a red substance called marrow. Marrow makes the red and white cells of the blood.

All bones have names of their own such as scapula (shoulder blade), patella (knee cap) and skull. There are 206 bones in the human body.

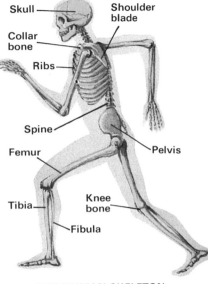

THE HUMAN SKELETON

Skull — Shoulder blade — Collar bone — Ribs — Spine — Femur — Pelvis — Tibia — Knee bone — Fibula

▼ The Gutenberg printing press.

BOOKS

Books are one of the most important inventions. All that we know, all the ideas, thoughts, beliefs and literature of the past can be found in books. We use them to learn from, for amusement and for inspiration.

The earliest known books were written by the Egyptians about 2500 BC. They were written on paper made from reeds and were rolled up to form a scroll. The Romans were the first to make modern-looking books.

They were inscribed by hand on parchment or vellum made from animal skin.

It was not until about 1439, when Johann Gutenberg invented his printing machine that movable type was used, and more than one book could be printed at a time. Today hundreds of thousands of books are printed every year.

See also GUTENBERG; PAPER;

BRAILLE
Braille is a form of writing used by blind people. A braille book has raised dots on its page instead of printed letters. The dots are arranged in patterns which represent letters or words. By touching the dots with their finger tips, blind people can read. They can also type in braille, using a machine which stamps out the dots through the paper.

▼ **The raised dots** which make braille words can be seen in this photograph.

The braille alphabet was invented by a Frenchman called Louis Braille. He lived from 1809 to 1852, and was blind from the age of three.

BRAIN
The brain and its extension, the spinal cord, are called the central nervous system.

The brain is divided into several different parts, each with its own job. One part, the *medulla*, controls breathing, heart rate and digestion, all of which you do without thinking. The *hypothalmus* controls the body's temperature and the amount of salt and water in the blood.

The largest part of the brain is the *cerebral cortex*. Different parts of the body are linked to different areas of the cortex. Sight, hearing and speech have their own areas, as do memory, thought and movement.

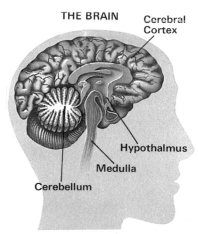

THE BRAIN
Cerebral Cortex
Hypothalmus
Medulla
Cerebellum

B

The spinal cord receives messages from the nerves and carries them to the brain. It also carries messages from the brain to the nerves. These connect with the muscles to make them work.

BRAZIL

This is the largest country in South America. It covers 8,511,000 square kilometres. The Equator crosses the north of Brazil. Just south of the Equator the mighty river Amazon flows from the Andes to the Atlantic.

The Amazon valley is a vast area of tropical plants and animals. Today many of the trees are being cut down, destroying this important natural area.

Most of Brazil's 135,564,000 people live in cities. It is the world's largest producer of coffee. Beef, cocoa, maize, sugar cane and tobacco are also produced. Oil has been discovered and there are many industries.

The Portuguese ruled Brazil from 1500 to 1825. It became a republic in 1889.

See also page 65.

BREATHING

All animals breathe. They need oxygen from the air to burn the food they eat and make energy.

Humans breathe through lungs. Lungs are spongy bags inside the body which fill with air when we breathe in. Oxygen from the air goes into the blood, and we breathe out carbon dioxide.

Fishes breathe through gills, which trap the oxygen dissolved in water. Insects breathe through tiny holes on the outside of their bodies. Plants take oxygen in through their leaves.

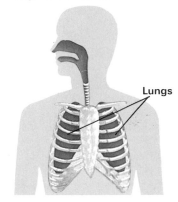

Lungs

▲ **Lungs expand** and contract as we breathe in and out.

BRIDGE

There are three basic types of bridge – *girder*, *arch* and *suspension*. These types can be combined in many ways and can be made of wood, stone, bricks, iron, concrete or steel.

The kind of bridge used for a site depends upon three factors: the hardness of the ground, the width and depth of the valley or

THREE KINDS OF BRIDGE

Girder: Winninger, Germany

38

river to be spanned and the weight to be carried.

The Romans built marvellous arch bridges, some of which still stand. Coalbrookdale, the first iron bridge, is an arch bridge. It was built in Britain in 1779.

The first major suspension bridge was the Menai Bridge in North Wales built by Thomas Telford in 1826. The longest suspension bridge is the Humber Estuary Bridge in the north-east of England.

▲ **A statue of Buddha** in a Bangkok temple.

BRONZE AGE

The Bronze Age followed the Stone Age. During this time, people used bronze instead of stone, flint, wood and bone for their weapons and tools.

Bronze is a mixture of copper and tin which can be hammered into many shapes to make weapons, tools and jewellery. It was used by the great early civilizations in the Middle East and Egypt. The Bronze Age lasted in Britain from 2500 BC until about 500 BC.

BUDDHA

Buddhism is one of the world's great religions. Its founder was Gautama, who lived from 563 to 483 BC. He was rich, yet he was sad for he knew the world was full of suffering. So he gave away his riches, and spent many years trying to find the answer to the world's unhappiness.

He taught that there are eight 'paths' to *nirvana*, or perfect peace. For this he was called Buddha, meaning 'Enlightened One', and today millions of Buddhists follow his teachings.

Arch:
Coalbrookdale, Britain

Suspension:
Golden Gate,
San Francisco, USA

39

BUFFALO

Buffalo are wild cattle of Africa and Asia. There are several kinds. The Indian water buffalo likes muddy swamps. It is a useful working animal, and also gives meat and milk. The African or Cape buffalo cannot be tamed. It has massive horns and can be very dangerous.

BULB

Plants make their own food, and some are able to store this food in special leaves called bulbs.

An onion is a bulb. When it is cut, you can see the closely packed layers of leaves. Daffodils, tulips and hyacinths also have bulbs. In spring they use food from the bulb to make new leaves.

BUTTERFLIES AND MOTHS

Butterflies are some of the most beautiful insects. They fly by day and their scaly wings are often brilliantly coloured. Most moths are less colourful. Moths usually fly at dusk. Butterflies and moths belong to the same family. Moths have hairier bodies, and they fold their wings flat when resting. Butterflies hold their wings upright instead.

Female butterflies and moths lay eggs which hatch into larvae called caterpillars. Caterpillars eat almost non-stop and grow by shedding their skins. Some, like that of the cabbage butterfly, are harmful to crops. Others, like the silkworm, are useful.

When the caterpillar is fully grown, it stops eating. It fastens itself to a leaf or twig and becomes a chrysalis. Inside the hard case of the chrysalis the caterpillar changes its shape. Soon the chrysalis splits and out crawls the adult insect. As soon as its wings are dry, it flies away.

BYZANTINE EMPIRE

In AD 330 the Roman Emperor Constantine made the city of Byzantium the capital of the eastern half of the Roman Empire. He renamed it Constantinople. It became the centre of the rich and powerful Byzantine Empire.

This empire became the storehouse of Greek learning and Roman law because it was not plundered by barbarians as Rome was after AD 500. It was here that the Greek Orthodox Church was formed.

The empire finally fell to the Turks in 1453.

▼ The scaly skin of a bulb protects the fleshy leaves inside.

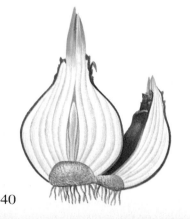

SOME BUTTERFLIES AND MOTHS

Peacock Butterfly

Swallowtail Butterfly

Small Copper Butterfly

Meadow Brown Butterfly

Common Blue Butterfly

Clouded Yellow Butterfly

Large White Butterfly

Puss Moth

Death's Head Hawkmoth

CAESAR, Julius (100–44 BC)

Julius Caesar was a Roman soldier, writer and statesman. He was a brilliant general. He conquered Gaul – what is today France, the Netherlands and Germany – and in 55 BC he invaded Britain. He wrote a book about his military experiences.

He disobeyed the Roman senate and brought his army back into Rome. He captured Rome and became dictator in 49 BC. Caesar had many enemies. They thought that he would make himself emperor, so they assassinated him on the Ides of March (the 15th) 44 BC.

See also ROME, ANCIENT.

CALCULATOR

Calculators are machines which help you to solve mathematical problems. One of the first calculators was the abacus, which was used in the Middle East over 5000 years ago. Today most calculators are electronic and work very fast indeed.

See also COMPUTER.

CALENDAR

A calendar is a way of dividing up the year into months, weeks and days. Practically everyone in the world uses the same kind of calendar. The Romans worked out our present calendar nearly 2000 years ago. They based it on the movements of the Earth around the Sun and the Moon around the Earth. In 1582, Pope Gregory XIII made some minor changes to the Roman calendar. This calendar, called the Gregorian calendar, is used today.

▼ **Camels** are a useful means of transport in North African countries.

CAMEL

For thousands of years this strange-looking animal has been used to carry people and their goods. The camel is well adapted to desert life. It stores fat in its hump and can go for days without water. Its wide, padded feet do not sink into the sand.

The Bactrian camel from Asia has two humps. It can live in quite cold regions. The Arabian camel has only one hump.

The light falls on to a strip of light-sensitive film, forming an image of the object.

When the film is treated with certain chemicals, or *developed*, the image shows up. The developed film is called a *negative*. The process of printing changes the negative image into a *positive* picture on specially coated paper. The result is a photograph. It may be in black and white or in colour depending on

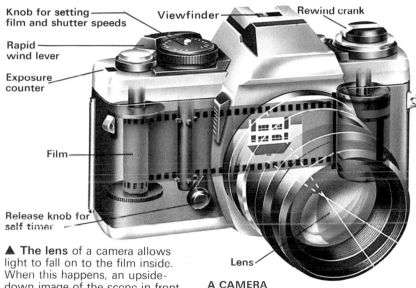

Knob for setting film and shutter speeds

Viewfinder

Rewind crank

Rapid wind lever

Exposure counter

Film

Release knob for self timer

▲ **The lens** of a camera allows light to fall on to the film inside. When this happens, an upside-down image of the scene in front of the lens (in this case a house) is formed on the film.

Lens

A CAMERA

CAMERA

A camera is a light-tight box with a window, or lens, on one side. When you take a picture, a shutter moves aside and lets light from the object you are photographing pass through the lens.

the type of film used.

To take a clear photo, the right amount of light must hit the film, and the lens must be focused to the distance from the object. Some cameras make these adjustments automatically. Others have controls to allow you to do it more accurately yourself.

CAMOUFLAGE

Many animals are coloured or shaped to match their background. We call this camouflage. Camouflage makes an animal difficult to see, and so protects it from enemies.

Spots or stripes help to hide an animal by breaking up the outline of its body. The zebra's stripes blend with the long grass on which it grazes. The leopard's spots conceal it among the sun-dappled leaves of a tree.

Most fishes have dark backs and light undersides. This makes them harder to see from above and from below. Many insects and reptiles are so well camouflaged that it is hard to spot them until they move.

Some animals trick their enemies by looking like something else. This is called *mimicry*. Leaf insects look like leaves, stick insects look like dead twigs. Some flies look like stinging wasps. Some harmless insects look like others which are poisonous or bad to eat.

CANADA

Canada is the second largest country in the world. Only Russia is bigger. Yet Canada has only about 25 million people. It covers the northern part of North America, stretching from the Atlantic Ocean in the east to the Pacific in the west and north to the Arctic Ocean. Canada's southern neighbour is the United States of America.

Canada is a land of high mountains, thick forests and vast plains. It has so many lakes and rivers that more than seven per cent of its area is made up of fresh water.

Because of its size Canada has a variety of climates. The west coast has cool summers and mild wet winters. On the plains and in the east the summers are hot and the winters cold. The north has short, cool summers and cold winters.

The land is very rich. The plains produce wheat and dairy products and timber comes from the forests. There are many minerals such as coal, oil, natural gas, gold and uranium. The rivers provide hydro-electricity.

▲ **Camouflage** is a useful means of protection for some animals. These insects use several techniques: the stick insect (4) and thorn tree hoppers (3) imitate pieces of twig. The leaf butterfly (2) and leaf insect (6) mimic leaves. The colour of the red underwing moth (1) and the bush cricket (7) matches their background while the pink orchard mantis (5) disguises itself as a flower.

Canada is divided into ten provinces and two territories. Each has its own government. But the federal (central) government in the capital, Ottawa, makes laws for all Canada. Canada is a member of the British Commonwealth.

See also page 65.

CANAL

Canals are man-made rivers. They are built to carry cargo boats, barges and ships. Canals have many other uses. They provide water for irrigating the land. In some low-lying countries they drain the land. And in Venice in Italy canals form the 'roads' of the city.

Some canals have been in use for a very long time. Parts of the Grand Canal in China are over 2000 years old. Today, the most important canals are the ship canals of Suez, Panama and the St Lawrence.

▲ **Mount Robson Park** in the Rockies, Canada.

CARBON

Carbon is one of the chemical elements. All living things contain carbon. If you hold a plate above a candle flame, a black deposit of carbon forms on it.

45

Both charcoal and coke are forms of carbon. The 'lead' in pencils and diamonds are natural forms of carbon.

CARTOON

Today cartoons are usually amusing films with animated talking animals, or strips in the newspapers and comic magazines. Originally, though, they were full-scale, detailed drawings made by artists as a kind of pattern for painting a picture or making a tapestry.

Besides being amusing, modern cartoons can also be comments upon an important event or personality of the day.

See also DISNEY.

CASTLE

Hundreds of years ago a castle was the safest place in time of war. The earliest castles were wooden forts. They were built on hill tops and surrounded by banks of earth and ditches. Inside there was room for the local people and their animals.

In the Middle Ages castles were built of stone. The outer walls were high and thick. There were towers along the walls, with slits through which archers could fire arrows. Around the walls was a ditch, or moat, filled with water. In the centre of the castle was a massive tower called a keep. Inside the keep, or in a separate building, was a great hall, where the nobleman and his family lived, and a chapel. Elsewhere in the castle were kitchens, storerooms, barracks for soldiers, stables for animals and a well.

It was difficult to capture a castle once the defenders had pulled up the drawbridge over the moat. Inside they had enough food and water to last for weeks. From the shelter of the castle

46

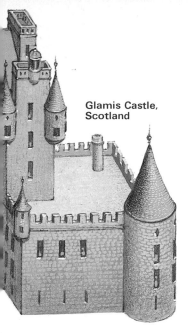

Glamis Castle, Scotland

CAT

A fluffy, playful kitten does not look very fierce. But it is a close relative of the mighty tiger. All cats are flesh-eating mammals. They hunt by stealth, usually alone. They move soundlessly because their claws retract into soft pads on their feet. They can see well, even at night, and they have a keen sense of smell.

Domestic cats are descended from the African wild cat. The

▼ **Four wild cats,** from left to right: a caracal, lynx, tiger and black panther.

▲ **Cartoon films** are made up of a series of still drawings, each showing a tiny part of the action.

walls they could shoot at the attackers, or drop boulders and boiling oil on top of them.

When an army laid siege to a castle, they surrounded the castle walls. If they failed to force their way in, they would try to starve the occupants out.

Although they must have been cold and damp to live in, castles were good strongholds until cannons were invented. Cannon balls easily smashed stone walls.

C

47

FIVE CAT BREEDS

Tortoiseshell
Short-hair

Russian Blue

Seal Point
Siamese

White Long-hair

Red
Long-hair

cat was sacred to the ancient Egyptians. In Europe cats did not become common mouse-hunters until the 1700s.

Cats make good pets. There are many kinds. But they are independent animals, and go back to living in the wild quite easily. The European wild cat looks like a large tabby, but it is very fierce.

Cats can breed twice a year. The female gives birth to five or six kittens. The young of the big cats, such as lions and tigers, are called cubs. All cats, even well-fed pets, are hunters, and the big cats are the fiercest hunters of all.

CATTLE
Cattle is the term applied to animals such as buffalo, bison and yaks, and bulls, oxen and cows.

Cattle are kept to supply milk, meat and hides. In many parts of Asia and Africa they are used to carry loads.

People have kept cattle since ancient times. Pictures of them appear in Egyptian tomb drawings and reliefs.

48

CAVE

Caves are found in the sides of hills and cliffs. They are hollowed out of the rock by the sea or by underground streams.

Some caves were used by early people as dwelling places and are very interesting to archaeologists. They often contain relics and fossils. See also STALACTITE & STALAGMITE.

CELL

All living things are made up of cells. Most cells can only be seen under a microscope.

The animal called an amoeba has only a single cell. But the human body has millions of cells, each with a job to do.

The centre of a cell is the nucleus; around the nucleus is a blob of jelly called protoplasm. Cells join together to make tissues – the materials of which our bodies are built. Different cells build skin, bone, blood, nerves, muscles and glands. Cells reproduce by dividing. In this way worn out cells are replaced by new cells as we grow.

Plants are also made up of cells. They have a thick cell wall, which gives them their stiffness.

CELTS

When we speak of Celts we are really talking about people who speak Celtic languages. They are not all alike physically.

The ancient Celts lived in north-western Europe. They had loosely organized tribes made up

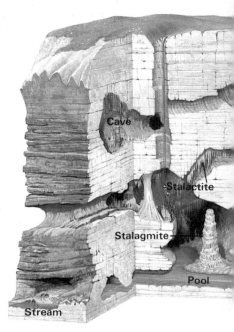

▲ **A section** through limestone showing caves hollowed out by streams. Notice the stalagmites and stalactites.

of a chief, nobles, free men and slaves. They were very warlike and fought among themselves. They were good metal workers and gifted musicians and poets. Their religion was Druidism.

Celts may have arrived in Britain as early as 600 BC. Later they were conquered by the Romans. Today the largest Celtic speaking groups are found in Ireland, Scotland and Wales.

CENTIPEDE & MILLEPEDE

Centipedes have rather flat, segmented bodies with one pair of legs on each segment. They hide

49

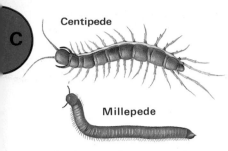
Centipede

Millepede

under logs and stones and come out at night to hunt. They run quickly and catch insects in their poisonous claws.

Millepedes have two pairs of legs on each segment of their bodies, but move more slowly than centipedes. They burrow into loose soil and eat rotting plants.

CEREALS
Cereals are important food crops. They belong to the grass family. The fruit or seed of the plant is called a grain.

In tropical lands the most important cereals are rice, maize and millet. In cooler climates the chief cereals are wheat, oats, barley and rye.

Rice is the main food for over half the people in the world. It grows in warm and wet climates and needs plenty of water.

Much of the world's wheat is grown on the plains of Canada, the USA, Australia and Russia. The grain is ground into flour and used to make bread, pasta and breakfast foods.

▼ **The world's** chief cereals.

Millet

Maize   Rice

CHAMELEON
Chameleons are African lizards. They catch insects by shooting out their long tongues. The chameleon can change colour to match its background. It does this as camouflage, to protect itself, or when it is angry.

CHARLEMAGNE (742–814)
The name Charlemagne means Charles the Great. He was king of a people called the Franks and he conquered and ruled a huge empire in Europe. This Christian

◄ **An international** chess tournament.

empire was the greatest since the time of Rome, and became known as the Holy Roman Empire.

Charlemagne and his warriors fought against many enemies, including the Moors in Spain. As well as being a great soldier, Charlemagne also built schools and libraries. Scholars from all over Europe came to his court.

Wheat   Rye   Barley

CHAUCER, Geoffrey
(1341–1400)
Chaucer was a great English poet whose most famous work is *The Canterbury Tales*. He was the first important author to write in English rather than Latin. *The Canterbury Tales* describes a group of people on a pilgrimage to the tomb of St Thomas à Becket at Canterbury. They entertain themselves by telling tales.

CHEESE
Cheese is made from the solid part, or curd, of sour milk.

Bacteria are added to milk to make it sour. The curd is then separated from the watery part, or whey. It is heated, pressed, cooled and stored until the cheese is ready.

There are many different kinds of cheese. Some famous English cheeses are Cheddar, Cheshire and Stilton. Cheeses such as Roquefort (France) and Gorgonzola (Italy), have blue veins in them. These are caused by special moulds.

CHEMISTRY
Chemistry is one of the main branches of science. The people who practise chemistry are called chemists. They look into the properties and make-up of matter. They try to find out what substances are made of, how they are put together, and how they react with other substances.

CHESS
This is a game which has been played for hundreds of years. It probably came from India where it was known in the 7th century. It spread from the east and had reached Europe by the 11th century.

Chess is played by two players on a board with 64 squares. Each player has 16 pieces which can only be moved in special ways. They attack, defend and can be captured and taken out of play. The king is the most important piece and the game is won when it is taken.

CHINA

China is the world's third largest country. About a fifth of the world's people are Chinese. For much of its history, China has been cut off from the rest of the world.

China became a united empire more than 2000 years ago. The land was ruled by royal families called dynasties. To keep out nomadic enemies, the emperor Shih Huang Ti built the Great Wall of China. Writing, music and painting flourished. Wise men studied the works of such teachers as Confucius and Lao Tse.

Cities and roads were built and merchants sailed as far as Africa and India. The Chinese invented paper and printing, and discovered how to make silk and gunpowder. Their fine pottery, or porcelain, was so famous that we still call all crockery 'china'.

For centuries the Chinese did not want anything to do with the outside world. But gradually China was made weak by civil wars and bad government. Europeans started trading in China in the 1800s and tried to run things for their own advantage. At first the Chinese were unable to stop them. Then, in the early 1900s, they overthrew the last of the emperors and set up a republic.

Later China was split by fighting between Communists and Nationalists. And during World War II Japan invaded China. By 1949, the Communists had won the civil war, and China, led by Mao Zedong, became a Communist state.

See also page 65.

▼ **Part of the Great Wall of China** built by the emperor Shih Huang Ti about 2000 years ago to keep out invaders from the north. It stretches for 3400 km.

▲ **A performing horse** in the circus ring.

CHURCH

Christians began to build churches when the Roman emperor Constantine was converted in the 4th century and they no longer had to worship in secret. These early buildings were patterned after the Roman basilica – an oblong hall with aisles and an apse, or rounded part, at the end. Later, a transept or two wings were often added to make the shape of a cross.

From the 5th to the 12th century many churches adopted the Romanesque style which had round arches and thick walls. In the Middle Ages the Gothic style appeared. This featured pointed spires, tall, narrow arches, richly stained glass windows and lots of stone carvings. Such churches were meant to inspire awe and wonder in the worshipper.

CHURCHILL, Winston Leonard Spencer (1874–1965)

Churchill was Prime Minister of Britain during World War II.

One of Churchill's ancestors was a great English general, the Duke of Marlborough (1650–1722). Churchill led an adventurous life as a soldier and newspaper reporter before becoming a politician. But his greatest years were from 1940 to 1945 when his stirring speeches and strong leadership encouraged people during the war against Hitler's Germany.

CIRCUS

The circus is a popular entertainment, often held inside a large tent. The circus show features clowns, acrobats, jugglers, trick riders and performing animals. There may be daring high wire walkers and trapeze fliers, as well as elephants, lions, sea lions, dogs and chimpanzees trained to do tricks.

In ancient Rome the circus was a huge race track. Thousands of people came to watch chariot races. The charioteers had to be strong and skilful to drive the horses round the tight bends of the track.

CITY

In prehistoric times people lived in groups for protection. They built a village with a wall or ditch around it. Gradually, some villages grew into towns. The most important towns or trade centres became the first cities.

Thousands of years ago the Egyptians built great cities. The ancient Greeks built Athens, with its beautiful temples. The city of Rome was the centre of the Roman Empire.

In the Middle Ages European cities such as London, Antwerp and Venice became rich through trade. But they were still small compared with cities today.

When the Industrial Revolution began in the 1700s, cities grew rapidly as people left the countryside to work in the new factories. Today cities are still growing as people arrive in search of jobs and better lives, and the largest cities have more people than many countries.

CIVIL WAR

A war fought between citizens of the same country is called a civil war. Sometimes a civil war marks a great change in a country's history.

▲ **Tokyo,** the capital of Japan, is the world's largest city.

In England the last civil war was fought from 1642 to 1649. It was a battle for power between the king, Charles I, and Parliament. Charles thought that he had a divine, or God-given, right to rule the country. Parliament thought he was too extravagant. Charles finally dismissed Parliament in 1642 and called his supporters to arms. They were called Royalists.

The parliamentary soldiers were the Roundheads. Led by Oliver Cromwell, they defeated the Royalists and captured the king. Charles was put on trial and executed in 1649. England became a monarchy once more in 1660, but the king never again had as much power as before the Civil War.

The American Civil War (1861–1865) was fought between the government (Union) backed by northern states, and the southern states (Confederacy). The war began when the southern states tried to break away from the North and form their own government. They wished to keep their slaves and creating their own government was one way of doing this. The Unionists won the Battle of Gettysburg in 1863 and began to win the war. The Confederate army surrendered in 1865.

In the last twenty years there have been many civil wars in Africa, Latin America and South-East Asia.

CIVILIZATION

Civilized people are able to develop arts, skills, trade and learning. Civilization began when people no longer had to spend all their time searching for food. Farming and trade developed as people settled in one area. As they grew more prosperous, they built cities, temples and roads. Most civilizations in ancient times had strong armies. Mighty empires spread their way of life by conquest.

Only the ruins of these great civilizations of the past now remain. But they have left their mark on our lives. Civilization in Europe today, for example, owes a great deal to the ideas of the Greeks and Romans. The modern world is a mixture of civilizations.

ANCIENT CIVILIZATIONS

C

Egypt   3000–500 BC

Crete   2500–1400 BC

Assyria   1912–612 BC

Babylonia   1900–538 BC

Phoenicia   1500–500 BC

Greece   1100–140 BC

Rome   753 BC–AD **470**

Persia   559–330 BC

CLEOPATRA (69–30 BC)

Cleopatra, Queen of Egypt, was one of the most beautiful and fascinating women in history. Two famous Roman rulers, Julius Caesar and Mark Antony, fell in love with her. Antony even gave parts of the Roman Empire to Cleopatra. The angry Romans made war on Antony, and defeated him. Antony killed himself, and Cleopatra also took her own life.

CLIMATE

Climate means the typical weather of a place over a long period of time.

Several factors affect climate. One is latitude – that is how far a place is from the Equator. The Sun's rays are most direct at the Equator, so it is hotter there. At the Poles the rays spread over a large land area and it is cool. A second factor is how close a place is to the sea. Water heats and cools more slowly than land. Away from the sea, land becomes much hotter in the summer and colder in winter.

The chief elements of climate are *temperature* and *rainfall*. The world's main climatic regions are based on average temperatures and rainfall figures measured over many years.

CLOCKS AND WATCHES

A clock is an instrument for measuring the time. A watch is a clock which is small enough to carry around.

Although the Chinese probably had clocks as early as AD 600, the earliest European clocks were made about 1200. They were made by blacksmiths and were often crude and clumsy. They used the force of gravity and were not very accurate.

A more accurate clock was developed when Galileo discovered that the pendulum could be used to measure time. From this time clocks have been improved and ordinary clocks are accurate to within a few minutes a year.

Today, two very precise clocks are used. One is the quartz crystal clock. The second is the caesium atomic clock which keeps time to within one second in 300 years.

See also GALILEO.

CLOUD

When it rains, the puddles soon dry. The water has turned into invisible water vapour.

The vapour rises into the air,

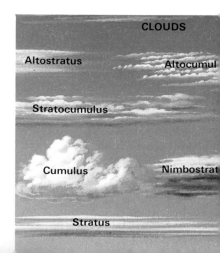

CLOUDS

Altostratus

Altocumul

Stratocumulus

Cumulus

Nimbostrat

Stratus

and the higher it rises, the cooler it becomes. As it cools, the vapour turns back into water. Millions of tiny drops of water, so light they float in the air, make clouds.

When the air can hold the water droplets no longer, they fall as rain. When the air is very cold, they turn to ice, and fall as hail or snow.

By studying the different kinds of cloud, scientists can tell what sort of weather to expect.

See also FOG; RAIN; WATER.

COAL

Coal is one of our most important fuels. It can be burned to heat buildings. At power stations it is burned to make electricity. Coal is also made into coal gas and coke, which are both good fuels. A lot of coke is used in the steel industry. Many chemicals can be produced from coal to make dyes, plastics, medicines and explosives.

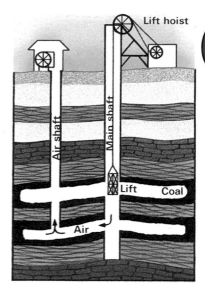

▲ **In a coal mine** shafts are dug down to the seams or workings. Miners travel down in a cage and fresh air is pumped down ventilation shafts.

Coal is mined from the ground. It is formed from the remains of forests of huge ferns and strange trees which grew millions of years ago. When these died, they became covered by mud and sand. In time the mud and sand changed into rocks. The dead plants were squeezed until they changed into coal. Most coal is deep underground and mining it is expensive and dangerous.

See also MINING.

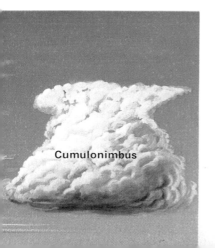

Cumulonimbus

◀ **Different types** of cloud bring different weather: cumulus clouds mean fine weather, low stratus clouds, rain. The cumulonimbus are thunder clouds.

▲ **A cocoa pod** may contain 40 beans.

COCOA

Cocoa comes from the seeds of the cacao tree, which is grown in West Africa, the West Indies and South America. The beans are dried, roasted and ground until a thick brown liquid forms. When squeezed and dried, this makes cocoa powder.

COFFEE

Coffee is made from the roasted and ground beans of the coffee plant. Coffee bushes grow best in warm, wet highland areas, such as in Brazil and Kenya. Inside each red berry are one or two beans. At harvest time, the beans are removed and dried in the sun. Then they are roasted until they are brown, and sold, either ground or whole.

COINS

Coins are small pieces of metal that have been issued by a government for use as money. Gold, silver, bronze, copper and various other alloys are used to make coins. They are made in a place called a mint. The first coins were made just before 600 BC in Asia Minor.

See also MONEY.

COLOUR

White light is actually a mixture of all colours. It is only when white light is split up, as it is in a rainbow, that we see its different colours.

The first person to understand light and colour was Sir Isaac Newton. In 1666, by passing light through a glass prism (a triangular solid block of glass), he obtained all the colours of a rainbow. This band of colour is called the spectrum. Newton then combined the colours again by passing them through a second prism to form white light.

The colours of the spectrum are always in the same order – red, orange, yellow, green, blue, indigo and violet.

We see the colour of a thing, such as a yellow flower, because all the other colours are taken in and only the yellow is reflected. A white flower gives back all the colours of light.

58

▲ The three primary light colours are red, green and blue. Other colours are made by mixing them.

▲ Mixing paints is different from mixing lights. You cannot make white by mixing coloured paints.

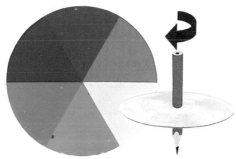

▲ White light is made up of a mixture of colours. You can see this if you spin a coloured top – the colours merge into white.

COLUMBUS, Christopher (1451–1506)

This Italian explorer discovered America by accident. He believed he could reach the Indies (Asia) by sailing west, instead of east, for he was sure the Earth was round. He persuaded the King of Spain to let him try, and in 1492 he set out with three ships, *Santa Maria, Pinta* and *Nina,* across the Atlantic Ocean. When he reached the Caribbean islands, Columbus thought he had reached Asia. So he called them the 'Indies'.

COMET

Comets are heavenly bodies. They are glowing balls of gas and dust which travel in an orbit, or path, around the Sun. Some of them have long tails. But they only start to glow when they get near the Sun. Some comets take only a few years to circle the Sun, others take thousands of years. The most famous comet is Halley's comet, which orbits the Sun every 77 years.

▲ **Comet Kahoutek**, first seen in 1973.

COMMONWEALTH

Most of the countries which were once part of the British Empire now belong to the Commonwealth of Nations. It includes huge countries, such as Australia, Canada and India, and tiny islands. Nearly all the members are self-governing, but their laws, schools and way of life are often similar. Some still trade mainly with Britain. The richer members try to help the poorer countries, and Commonwealth leaders meet regularly to discuss their economic and financial problems.

COMMUNISM

In a 'commune' people share everything they have. The main idea behind Communism is that wealth should be shared. So Communist governments control all factories, mines, farms and shops.

Karl Marx and Friedrich Engels put forward Communist ideas in the 1800s, after the Industrial Revolution. The first country to have a Communist government was Russia, after the 1917 revolution. Later, much of eastern Europe and Cuba also became Communist. So did China, although its ideas about Communism are different from those of Russia.

▲ **A compass needle** always points north.

COMPASS

A compass is an instrument used to find directions. A simple compass has a needle which always points in the same directions — north and south. This kind of compass is a magnetic compass. It does this because the Earth itself is a big magnet. The compass lines up parallel with the Earth's magnetic field.

C

Most ships and planes use a gyrocompass. This device contains a spinning drum and, once set, its axis always points in one direction, no matter which way the ship or plane turns.

COMPUTER

Computers are electronic machines like calculators. But computers do more than work out mathematical problems. They can *process* information. This means that they can be given information, store it and sort through it in order to carry out a task. What is more they can work at incredible speeds.

Computers cannot think. They have to have instructions called *programs* to tell them what to do with the information they are given. These programs can be changed so that computers can do an enormous number of different things. Today they are found in offices, hospitals, factories and schools. They can send spacecraft to outer planets, help

▲ **A mainframe computer** consists of several large units – the input station, central processor, memory stores, and output units such as printers.

forecast the weather, run machines and play exciting games.

Every computer has four main parts. The *input* is where the computer receives instructions and information; the *central processing unit* (CPU) is where calculations arc carried out; the *memory* is where information and instructions are stored and the *output* is where the result is displayed.

The first computer ENIAC was built in 1946. It filled a whole room. Today the programs to run a computer can be held electronically on tiny silicon chips and computers are much smaller. The largest are called mainframes and the smallest are called micros. In between come the minicomputers.

See also CALCULATOR; ELECTRONICS; SILICON CHIP.

CONSERVATION

Conservation is the protection of nature, including natural resources such as water, soil, minerals, forests and wildlife.

For centuries people have made use of these resources without any thought of preserving them. Conservationists work to prevent the pollution of our earth, air and water and the destruction of rare animals.

CONSTELLATION

From earliest times people have studied the night sky. It did not take them long to realize that the sky had a systematic pattern. The stars were in fixed groups, or constellations. People saw the shapes of animals and the heroes of their myths and named groups of stars after them.

Some constellations always come up in the east in a certain order just before sunrise and seem to travel in the same path as the Sun. These are the twelve figures or signs of the zodiac.

There are 88 constellations. The Greeks identified and named 48 of them. Some can be seen only in the northern hemisphere and some only in the southern hemisphere.

See also ASTRONOMY; STARS; UNIVERSE.

COOK, Captain James
(1728–1779)

James Cook made three voyages of discovery to the Pacific and Antarctic oceans.

The first was an expedition to the South Seas in 1768. He sailed to Tahiti and then to New Zealand. In 1770 he reached Botany Bay in Australia and claimed it for Britain.

On his second voyage (1772–1775), he sailed 120,000 kilometres, going right round the world. On his third expedition he discovered the Hawaiian Islands. He was killed there by natives.

See also EXPLORERS.

▼ **This map** traces the Sun's path against the constellations of the Zodiac. The yellow circles mark its position on the first of each month.

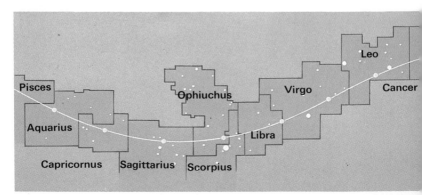

COPERNICUS, Nicolaus
(1473–1543)

Copernicus was a Polish astronomer. He showed that the Earth was not the centre of the Universe. He stated that the Earth revolves once every 24 hours, that it travels round the Sun once a year and that it and the other planets form the Solar System.

See also ASTRONOMY.

COPPER

Copper was one of the first metals to be used. To begin with people used pure copper which they found on the ground. But they later learned how to extract it from ore by smelting.

Pure copper is very soft. It is often mixed with other metals to make a harder alloy like brass.

See also METAL.

CORTES, Hernando
(1485–1547)

Cortes was a Spanish soldier who conquered the Aztec Empire in Mexico between 1519 and 1521

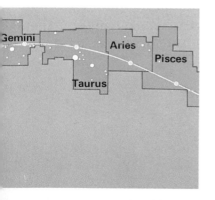

with less than 600 men. Cortes also had guns and therefore great power over the people as they thought he was a god. He ruled as governor until 1530.

▲ **These fluffy** bolls of cotton will be cleaned by a machine called a gin, and pressed into bales.

COTTON

Cotton is a very useful plant. Inside its round fruits, called bolls, are masses of white fibres. When the fruits ripen, they split and the fibres are blown away, spreading the seeds. But in the cotton fields, the bolls are picked before this can happen.

Cotton grows best in warm, wet lands. It is grown in the USSR, southern United States, India, China, Egypt and Brazil.

See also SPINNING AND WEAVING.

COUNTRIES OF THE WORLD

C There are over 160 independent countries in the world. They vary enormously in size, from the Vatican City (the world's smallest country) to the world's largest country — the USSR.

The table on these pages shows all of the independent countries of the world with their capital cities and population.

EUROPE

Country	Population	Capital
Albania	2,962,000	Tirana
Andorra	39,000	Andorra la Vella
Austria	7,555,000	Vienna
Belgium	9,903,000	Brussels
Bulgaria	8,957,000	Sofia
Cyprus	665,000	Nicosia
Czechoslovakia	15,500,000	Prague
Denmark	5,114,000	Copenhagen
Finland	4,908,000	Helsinki
France	54,621,000	Paris
Germany, East	16,644,000	East Berlin
Germany, West	61,015,000	Bonn
Greece	9,878,000	Athens
Hungary	10,643,000	Budapest
Iceland	241,000	Reykjavik
Ireland	3,552,000	Dublin
Italy	57,128,000	Rome
Liechtenstein	28,000	Vaduz
Luxembourg	366,000	Luxembourg
Malta	383,000	Valletta
Monaco	28,000	Monaco
Netherlands	14,484,000	Amsterdam
Norway	4,152,000	Oslo
Poland	37,203,000	Warsaw
Portugal	10,229,000	Lisbon
Romania	23,017,000	Bucharest
San Marino	22,000	San Marino
Spain	38,602,000	Madrid
Sweden	8,350,000	Stockholm
Switzerland	6,482,000	Bern
Turkey	49,272,000	Ankara
United Kingdom	56,125,000	London
USSR	278,618,000	Moscow
Vatican City	1,000	Vatican City
Yugoslavia	23,123,000	Belgrade

AFRICA

Country	Population	Capital
Algeria	21,718,000	Algiers
Angola	8,754,000	Luanda
Benin	3,932,000	Porto Novo
Botswana	1,085,000	Gaborone
Burkina Faso	6,639,000	Ouagadougou
Burundi	4,718,000	Bujumbura
Cameroon	9,873,000	Yaounde
Cape Verde Is.	326,000	Praia
Central African Republic	2,608,000	Bangui
Chad	5,018,000	N'djamena
Comoros	444,000	Moroni
Congo	1,740,000	Brazzaville
Djibouti	430,000	Djibouti
Egypt	48,503,000	Cairo
Equatorial Guinea	392,000	Malabo
Ethiopia	43,350,000	Addis Ababa
Gabon	1,151,000	Libreville
Gambia	643,000	Banjul
Ghana	13,588,000	Accra
Guinea	6,075,000	Conakry
Guinea-Bissau	890,000	Bissau
Ivory Coast	9,810,000	Abidjan
Kenya	20,333,000	Nairobi
Lesotho	1,528,000	Maseru
Liberia	2,189,000	Monrovia
Libya	3,605,000	Tripoli
Madagascar	9,985,000	Antananarivo
Malawi	7,059,000	Lilongwe
Mali	8,206,000	Bamako
Mauritania	1,888,000	Nouakchott
Mauritius	1,021,000	Port Louis
Morocco	21,941,000	Rabat
Mozambique	13,961,000	Maputo
Namibia	1,100,000	Windhoek
Niger	6,115,000	Niamey
Nigeria	95,198,000	Lagos
Rwanda	6,070,000	Kigali
São Tomé & Príncipe	108,000	São Tomé
Senegal	6,444,000	Dakar
Seychelles	65,000	Victoria
Sierra Leone	3,602,000	Freetown
Somali Republic	4,653,000	Mogadishu
South Africa	32,392,000	Pretoria
Sudan	21,550,000	Khartoum
Swaziland	647,000	Mbabane
Tanzania	21,733,000	Dodoma
Togo	2,960,000	Lomé
Tunisia	7,081,000	Tunis
Uganda	15,477,000	Kampala
Zaire	30,363,000	Kinshasa
Zambia	6,666,000	Lusaka
Zimbabwe	8,300,000	Harare

ASIA

Country	Population	Capital
Afghanistan	18,136,000	Kabul
Bahrain	417,000	Manama
Bangladesh	98,657,000	Dacca
Bhutan	1,417,000	Thimphu
Brunei	224,000	Bandar Seri Begawan
Burma	37,153,000	Rangoon
Cambodia	7,284,000	Phnom Penh
China	1,060,000,000	Beijing (Peking)
Hong Kong	5,398,000	Victoria
India	750,900,000	Delhi
Indonesia	163,393,000	Djakarta
Iran	44,632,000	Tehran
Iraq	15,898,000	Baghdad
Israel	4,233,000	Jerusalem
Japan	120,754,000	Tokyo
Jordan	3,515,000	Amman
Korea (N)	19,500,000	Pyongyang
Korea (S)	41,999,000	Seoul
Kuwait	1,710,000	Kuwait
Laos	4,117,000	Vientiane
Lebanon	2,668,000	Beirut
Malaysia	15,577,000	Kuala Lumpur
Maldives	177,000	Malé
Mongolia	1,891,000	Ulan Bator
Nepal	16,625,000	Katmandu
Oman	1,242,000	Muscat
Pakistan	96,180,000	Islamabad
Philippines	54,378,000	Manila
Qatar	315,000	Doha
Saudi Arabia	11,542,000	Riyadh
Singapore	2,558,000	Singapore
Sri Lanka	15,837,000	Colombo
Syria	10,267,000	Damascus
Taiwan	19,600,000	Taipei
Thailand	51,301,000	Bangkok
Turkey	49,272,000	Ankara
United Arab Emirates	1,327,000	Abu Dhabi
USSR	278,618,000	Moscow
Vietnam	59,713,000	Hanoi
North Yemen AR	6,849,000	San'a
South Yemen PDR	2,294,000	Aden

SOUTH AMERICA

Country	Population	Capital
Argentina	30,564,000	Buenos Aires
Bolivia	6,429,000	La Paz
Brazil	135,564,000	Brasilia
Chile	12,074,000	Santiago
Colombia	28,624,000	Bogotá
Ecuador	9,378,000	Quito
French Guiana	79,000	Cayenne
Guyana	790,000	Georgetown
Paraguay	3,681,000	Asunción
Peru	19,698,000	Lima
Surinam	375,000	Paramaribo
Uruguay	3,012,000	Montevideo
Venezuela	17,317,000	Caracas

NORTH AND CENTRAL AMERICA THE WEST INDIES

Country	Population	Capital
Anguilla (Br.)	7,000	The Valley
Antigua and Barbuda	80,000	St John's
Bahamas	231,000	Nassau
Barbados	253,000	Bridgetown
Belize	166,000	Belmopan
Bermuda	78,000	Hamilton
Canada	25,379,000	Ottawa
Costa Rica	2,600,000	San José
Cuba	10,099,000	Havana
Dominica	76,000	Roseau
Dominican Republic	6,243,000	Santo Domingo
El Salvador	4,819,000	San Salvador
Greenland (Dan.)	54,000	Godthaab
Grenada	112,000	St George's
Guadeloupe (Fr.)	334,000	Basse-Terre
Guatemala	7,963,000	Guatemala City
Haiti	6,585,000	Port-au-Prince
Honduras	4,372,000	Tegucigalpa
Jamaica	2,337,000	Kingston
Martinique (Fr.)	329,000	Fort-de-France
Mexico	78,524,000	Mexico City
Nicaragua	3,272,000	Managua
Panama	2,180,000	Panama City
Puerto Rico (US)	3,300,000	San Juan
St Kitts-Nevis	46,000	Basseterre
St Lucia	130,000	Castries
St Vincent and the Grenadines	104,000	Kingstown
Trinidad & Tobago	1,185,000	Port-of-Spain
United States of America	239,283,000	Washington DC

AUSTRALASIA

Country	Population	Capital
Australia	15,752,000	Canberra
Fiji	696,000	Suva
Kiribati	63,000	Tarawa
Nauru	8,000	Nauru
New Caledonia	171,000	Nouméa
New Zealand	3,254,000	Wellington
Niue	4,000	Alofi
Papua New Guinea	3,300,000	Moresby
Solomon Islands	270,000	Honiara
Tonga	105,000	Nuku'alofa
Tuvalu	8,000	Funafuti
Vanuatu	142,000	Port Vila
Western Samoa	163,000	Apia

C

TROPIC OF CANCER

EQUATOR

TROPIC OF CAPRICORN

Greenland

ICELAND

Alaska
(USA)

C A N A D A

IRELAND

UNITED STATES
OF AMERICA

PORTUGAL

SP

MOROCCO

MEXICO

BAHAMAS

CUBA

PUERTO RICO
DOMINICA
ST LUCIA

MAURITANIA

CAPE·
VERDE
ISLANDS

46

53

54 55

56

57

47

52

48

50

VENEZUELA

58

59 60

49

51

COLOMBIA

ECUADOR

PERU

BRAZIL

BOLIVIA

PARAGUAY

URUGUAY

ARGENTINA

Falkland Islands

26

27

28

29

30

31

IVORY COAST

1 DENMARK	11 YUGOSLAVIA	21 NORTH YEMEN A.
2 NETHERLANDS	12 ALBANIA	22 BHUTAN
3 BELGIUM	13 CYPRUS	23 BANGLADESH
4 LUXEMBOURG	14 LEBANON	24 CAMBODIA
5 W. GERMANY	15 ISRAEL	25 TUNISIA
6 E. GERMANY	16 SYRIA	26 SENEGAL
7 SWITZERLAND	17 JORDAN	27 GAMBIA
8 AUSTRIA	18 KUWAIT	28 GUINEA-BISSAU
9 CZECHOSLOVAKIA	19 BAHRAIN	29 GUINEA
10 HUNGARY	20 UNITED ARAB EMIRATES	30 SIERRA LEONE

31 LIBERIA
32 BURKINA FASO
33 TOGO
34 CENTRAL AFRICAN REPUBLIC
35 EQUATORIAL GUINEA
36 GABON
37 CAMEROON
38 UGANDA
39 RWANDA
40 BURUNDI

41 DJIBOUTI
42 MALAWI
43 ZIMBABWE
44 SWAZILAND
45 LESOTHO
46 BELIZE
47 GUATEMALA
48 HONDURAS
49 EL SALVADOR
50 NICARAGUA

51 COSTA RICA
52 PANAMA
53 JAMAICA
54 HAITI
55 DOMINICAN REPUBLIC
56 BARBADOS
57 TRINIDAD AND TOBAGO
58 GUYANA
59 SURINAM
60 FRENCH GUIANA

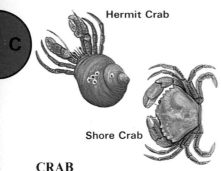

Hermit Crab

Shore Crab

CRAB

Along with shrimps, prawns and lobsters, crabs belong to the group of animals called crustaceans.

Most crabs live in the sea. They have jointed legs, like insects, and walk sideways. They seize food in their strong pincers, or claws.

There are about 5000 kinds of crabs. They vary in size from tiny pea crabs less than a centimetre across to giant crabs measuring 30 centimetres or more.

CRICKET

The game of cricket began in the 1800s. It is played by two teams of 11 players, using a wooden bat and a leather ball. Each team takes it in turn to 'bat' and to 'field'. The batsmen try to score 'runs' by hitting the ball when it is bowled to them. The bowler, helped by fielders, tries to get the batsmen 'out'.

CROCODILE & ALLIGATOR

These reptiles are related. They both have tough, armoured skin and their ears, eyes and nostrils are located at the top of their heads. Unlike most reptiles, crocodiles and alligators lay their eggs in a nest or heap of dead leaves and plants. As the plants rot they provide heat which helps to hatch the eggs.

Crocodiles live in Africa, Asia and Australia. They eat mostly fish, turtles, birds and water mammals. They vary in size from $1\frac{1}{2}$ to 6 metres and they have narrow, pointed heads.

Alligators live in America and China where they can grow as large as crocodiles. They eat mostly fish.

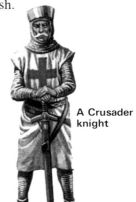

A Crusader knight

CROMWELL, Oliver
(1599–1658)

Cromwell was one of the most famous men in English history. He helped to lead Parliament's army to victory over the Royalists in the Civil War and later became Lord Protector from 1653 to 1658. He was one of those who signed the warrant for the execution of Charles I.

See also CIVIL WAR.

CRUSADES

The Crusades were wars in which Christian armies fought to win back the Holy Land of Palestine from the Muslims.

The First Crusade began in 1096 after Pope Urban II had called on the Christians of Europe to capture Jerusalem, which was a sacred city to the Muslims, too. Many knights answered the call, and the First Crusade was a great success. The crusaders captured Jerusalem in 1099. But the Muslims were not beaten. In 1187, led by the great sultan Saladin, they recaptured Jerusalem.

There were eight Crusades in all. Thousands of crusaders went to the Holy Land. Before the Muslims finally defeated them in 1303, many crusaders had died of sickness or in battle.

▲ **The Nile crocodile** lives in Africa. The bird on its back is looking for parasites to eat.

The Crusades brought Europeans into contact with the way of life of the East. They learned Eastern medicine and science, and were encouraged to trade for the riches of the East.

CRYSTAL

If you look closely at sugar, you will see that it is made up of thousands of tiny glassy pieces with flat sides. These are sugar crystals.

All crystals have a definite shape. They have smooth, flat sides that meet in sharp corners. There are many different varieties of crystal shapes and sizes. Many crystals are so beautiful and hard that they are used as gems in jewellery.

▲ **Pierre and Marie Curie** in their laboratory.

CUCKOO

The cuckoo of Europe does not build its own nest. Instead, it lays its egg in the nest of another bird.

When the young cuckoo hatches, it pushes out the other eggs and nestlings. The foster-parents do not seem to notice. They feed the cuckoo until it is bigger than they are. Finally the cuckoo flies away. Cuckoos go to Africa in winter and return to Europe in spring.

CURIE, Marie (1867–1934) and Pierre (1859–1906)

The Curies were among the earliest workers in the science of radioactivity. Radioactivity has to do with the powerful rays given off by some rare materials.

In 1898 the Curies discovered and worked on both polonium and radium. They shared a Nobel prize in physics in 1903 with Henri Becquerel for their work on radioactivity.

Madame Curie was awarded a second Nobel prize in chemistry in 1911 for her further work on radium.

See also RADIOACTIVITY.

CYCLONE

A cyclone is a storm in which the wind circles or spirals inward about a low-pressure area. The winds can be very strong – up to 240 kilometres an hour – and there is often torrential rain, causing floods. Yet the centre or 'eye' of the storm is quite calm.

Cyclones often begin over water. When they hit the land they cause great damage. Houses may be blown down, trees up-rooted and crops damaged.

▼ **The baby cuckoo** soon grows larger than its foster parents.

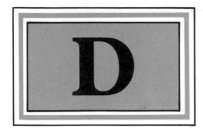

D

DAM
A dam is a barrier built across a river or lake. Some dams are built to create a reservoir for storing water, others to control flooding or to produce water power for making electricity.

DARWIN, Charles Robert
(1809–1882)
Darwin was a great naturalist whose theory of evolution sought to explain why there are so many different kinds of plants and animals. Darwin said that those animals and plants whose slight differences made them better able to live in their environment would survive and pass on their differences to their offspring.

Darwin put forward this idea of natural selection in his *Origin of Species* in 1859.

▲ **Two red deer** stags fighting over a herd of females.

The New Cornelia Tailings Dam, USA, is the world's biggest dam. It contains over 200 million cubic metres of earth and rock. Other dams are giant slabs of concrete. The Grand Coulee Dam in Washington state, USA, is the biggest concrete dam. It holds back the water by its sheer weight. Other concrete dams are strong because of their shape, which is arched towards the flow of water.

DEER
Deer are hoofed mammals, which run swiftly to escape their enemies. Like antelope and cattle, deer chew the cud. Usually only the stags (males) have horns, or antlers. Females are called hinds.

Deer live in cooler climates than antelopes. Most deer live in woodland, feeding on grass and leaves. The reindeer, or caribou, lives on the cold northern tundra. The largest deer is the moose or elk of North America and Europe.

DEMOCRACY

The word *democracy* comes from two Greek words and means 'government by the people'. In ancient times emperors and kings had great power to make laws and collect taxes. In a democracy a group of men and women elected by the people make the laws.

Some democracies are republics. The head of state is an

Most deserts are in the middle of continents. There is little rain, because the moist winds from the sea are dry by the time they reach these deserts. Because there are no clouds, a desert may get very hot during the day. But at night, the dry soil quickly loses its heat and the desert becomes cold.

Strong winds blow away the soil, leaving bare rock, or sweep the sand into great waves called

elected president. But some still have a king or queen, although the country is governed by parliament.

If the people living in a democracy do not like the government, they vote against it at an election. The political parties put forward their ideas.

DESERT

Not all deserts are hot and sandy. Some are cold. Many are rocky. But all get very little rain and snow. About a fifth of the Earth's land surface is desert.

▲ **In the deserts** of the Middle East, nomads pass by on camels. In the distance is an oasis where there is water.

dunes. It is difficult for plants to live in such conditions. Many desert animals shelter from the sun by day and come out only at night. Some never drink, but get all the moisture they need from their food.

The world's largest desert is the Sahara in Africa. There are other huge deserts in central Asia (the Gobi), in southern Africa, Australia, India, and in North and South America.

DIAMOND

Diamonds are our most precious gems. They are cut from crystals which are found in rocks. Diamonds are a form of carbon. If expertly cut, they sparkle with reflected light. Diamonds are expensive because they are rare and difficult to cut. They are the hardest of all the minerals. Some diamonds are made into cutting tools for industry.

DICKENS, Charles John Huffam (1812–1870)

Dickens is one of the greatest English novelists. He created many famous characters, like the miser Scrooge in *A Christmas Carol*, and often wrote about children. In *David Copperfield* he described his own boyhood. Though his books contain many humorous characters, they also tell of the poverty, crime and cruelty of his day. Dickens' writing encouraged people to do something about these problems.

DIGESTION

The food we eat must be changed by the body before it can be absorbed by the blood and used to nourish the cells of the body. Food is changed into nourishment by the digestive system.

Digestion begins in the mouth where food is chewed into small pieces and mixed with saliva before being pushed down into the stomach. The stomach churns the food, mixing it with gastric juice, and turns it into a soft paste which passes slowly into the small intestine.

Inside the small intestine it is further broken down by being mixed with bile from the liver and juice from the pancreas. Much of this fluid passes through the wall of the small intestine into the blood. The waste passes into the large intestine and leaves the body as faeces.

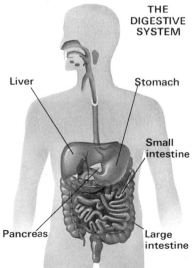

THE DIGESTIVE SYSTEM

Liver

Stomach

Small intestine

Pancreas

Large intestine

DINOSAUR

Millions of years ago, long before people lived on Earth, the mighty dinosaurs ruled the animal kingdom.

The word *dinosaur* means 'the terrible lizard'. The dinosaurs were reptiles, and some of them were the largest land animals that have ever lived. The first dinosaur appeared about 200 million years ago; the last dinosaurs died out about 65 million years ago, but we know something of what they looked like from their fossil remains in the rocks. Some were quite small, but others were huge. There were plant-eating and flesh-eating dinosaurs.

Among the plant-eaters were the biggest dinosaurs, such as *Brachiosaurus* and *Diplodocus*. They walked on four thick legs, and had long necks and tails.

Some giant dinosaurs were nearly 30 metres long. Others weighed 80 tonnes.

Flesh-eating dinosaurs were smaller and most of them ran on their hind legs. The largest and fiercest was *Tyrannosaurus*, the 'tyrant lizard'. It stood 5½ metres high and weighed 7 tonnes. It had huge sharp claws and long sharp teeth.

Despite their great size and strength, dinosaurs had tiny brains. When they died out, mammals, which until then had been unimportant little animals, took their place. Scientists are not sure why dinosaurs became extinct. Perhaps the climate became cooler, and the vegetation changed, so that the dinosaurs could not keep warm or get enough food.

See also FOSSIL; PREHISTORIC ANIMALS.

DISEASE

When something goes wrong with part of your body, you may have a disease.

Many diseases are *infectious*. They are caused by attacks on the body by tiny living things. Bacteria cause diseases such as typhoid and tuberculosis. Viruses give us influenza, measles and the common cold.

Diseases can also be caused by poor diet and lack of vitamins. Sometimes glands can go wrong and upset the body. Some diseases are *hereditary*. This means they can be passed on from parents to children.

Drugs can cure many diseases. And vaccination can protect us from others.

See also BACTERIA; DRUGS; MEDICINE; VITAMIN.

DISNEY, Walt (1901–1966)

Walt Disney opened a motion picture animation studio in 1923 and by 1928 he had made his first short talking film which starred Mickey Mouse.

Disney's first full-length cartoon film was *Snow White and the Seven Dwarfs*. Other cartoon films included *Bambi*, *Pinocchio*, *Dumbo* and *Cinderella*. He also made real-life films.

See also CARTOON.

◀ **A scene** from over 100 million years ago. The *Tyrannosaurus* attacks its plant-eating prey, the *Corythosaurus*. Behind them an armoured *Ankylosaurus* grazes.

DIVING

To remain underwater for more than a few minutes, divers must wear breathing apparatus. In fairly shallow waters divers use a device called an aqualung. It supplies them with compressed air through a mouthpiece. Deep sea divers wear a special pressure suit pumped up with air.

DODO

The dodo was a flightless bird which lived on the island of Mauritius in the Indian Ocean. The dodo was clumsy and helpless, but it had no natural enemies. Then sailors brought dogs, pigs and rats to the island. The dodos were killed and their eggs eaten. The last dodo died in 1681.

▼ **A diver** preparing to launch a diving bell, a special diving vessel for exploring below 200 metres.

SIX DOG BREEDS

Springer spaniel

Bulldog

Toy poodle

Greyhound

Scottish terrier

Pekinese

DOG

The dog was the first animal to be tamed by human beings. Cave men probably reared wild dog pups and trained them to hunt.

Today, there are many different breeds, or kinds, of dog. Dogs used for hunting are called *sporting dogs*. Terriers, hounds, spaniels, setters, pointers and retrievers are sporting dogs.

Working dogs do many useful jobs. Huskies, sheepdogs, alsatians and St Bernards do a variety of jobs for man.

Even though the dog has lived close to people for so long, it still has the instincts of a wild animal. Before going to sleep, a dog will turn round and round – as if making a bed in dry leaves. Because wild dogs live in packs, or groups, the dog's instinct is to follow and obey the pack leader. This makes it easy to train. Its master becomes the 'pack leader'.

The wild members of the dog family include coyotes, foxes, jackals and hunting dogs.

DOLPHIN

Dolphins are small whales. They live in the sea or in big rivers, and they eat fish. Dolphins are mammals, so they have to come to the surface to breathe. They are marvellous swimmers and often play by leaping right out of the water and twisting about.

DRAGON

A dragon is a fabulous monster. It is represented as a gigantic reptile having a lion's claws, the tail of a serpent, wings and a scaly skin. It often breathes fire.

Mostly we think of dragons as being evil, fearful creatures, but this is not always so. The Chinese think the sign of a dragon can protect them from evil or injury.

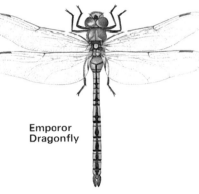

Emporor Dragonfly

DRAGONFLY

The dragonfly is one of the fastest flying insects. It lays its eggs in ponds and rivers. The young dragonfly, or larva, lives underwater. When fully grown, it climbs up a plant stem to shed its skin and become an adult.

▲ Dolphins are playful, intelligent marine mammals.

DRUGS

Herbs and chemicals that are used to cure diseases are called drugs. Some mosses and herbs contain healing substances, which have been known to people since earliest times. By the 1600s nearly every town had an apothecary, or chemist, who made up pills and mixtures. Many of these did no good at all.

In the 1800s the first man-made drugs, produced from chemicals, were used. A great step forward was the discovery of penicillin in 1928. This was the first *antibiotic* drug, which could kill harmful bacteria.

Drugs can be dangerous if they are not used properly. People can become addicted to certain drugs; this means they cannot live without them.

See also DISEASE.

77

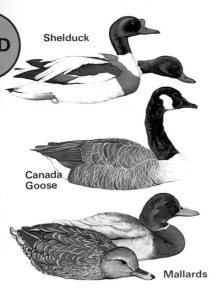

Shelduck

Canada Goose

Mallards

DUCKS AND GEESE

Ducks are swimming birds, with short legs and webbed feet. They live on lakes and rivers or on marshes or the sea. Male ducks are called drakes. They are often more colourful than females. There are many different kinds of duck.

Geese look rather like large ducks with long necks. They spend much of their time on land, nibbling grass or other plant food. The male goose is called a gander. Wild ducks and geese often migrate for long distances.

DYE

Dyes are substances used to colour fabrics and other materials. Some dyes come from plants and animals. A red dye called madder comes from the roots of the madder plant. Cochineal is a scarlet dye obtained from the cochineal insect. But most of the dyes used these days are made from chemicals. Many of these man-made dyes have brilliant colours.

DYNAMITE

In 1866 Alfred Nobel, a Swedish chemist, accidentally made an important discovery. He mixed a very dangerous explosive called nitro-glycerine with a kind of sandy earth called kieselguhr. It became a solid cheesy substance which could be handled safely but was still a powerful explosive. He called it dynamite.

Nobel made a fortune from explosives. With some of the funds he set up a fund to give yearly prizes to scientists and writers whose work has helped mankind. These are known as Nobel Prizes.

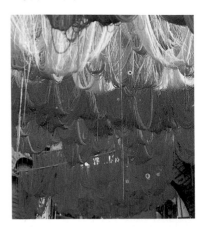

▲ Dyed wool hanging in a Moroccan market.

E

◄ The golden eagle has a wingspan of 2.3 metres. It lives in mountainous areas.

EAGLE

These fierce birds of prey are the kings of the bird world. Some types may have a wingspan of more than two metres. Eagles can fly to great heights. The largest eagles can carry off lambs and even young deer in their strong claws.

Today, eagles are protected by law. Eagles are becoming rare because people have shot and poisoned many of them.

EAR

Any sound causes vibrations which are passed by the *outer ear* down to the ear drum. The ear drum then vibrates, just like the skin of a musical drum. Three tiny bones in the *middle ear* pick up and pass on the vibrations. Inside the *inner ear* is a shell-like tube full of fluid. The vibrating air makes the fluid vibrate too. Nerves send messages about the vibrations to the brain. And when the brain has worked out what the messages mean, we 'hear' the sounds.

The inner ear also helps us keep our balance by mean of fluid-filled tubes.

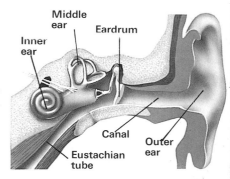

▲ A cutaway drawing of an ear.

79

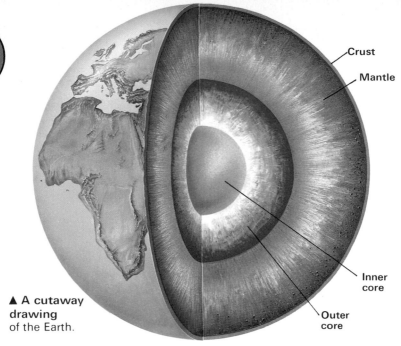

Crust
Mantle
Inner core
Outer core

▲ A cutaway drawing of the Earth.

EARTH

The Earth we live on is one of nine planets which orbit the Sun. Scientists think the Earth was probably formed from a spinning cloud of gas and dust. From the age of the oldest rocks we know that the Earth is more than 4000 million years old.

The Earth has an invisible outer covering called the atmosphere. The atmosphere lies in several layers. The outer edge is about 1600 kilometres from the Earth. The lowest layer, the *troposphere*, is where life exists.

The Earth is the only planet with large amounts of surface water. Oceans and seas cover 70 per cent of its surface. The water was formed by chemical reactions after the Earth had become a solid ball of rock.

The Earth is rocky, and very rugged in places. It is made up of igneous, or crystallized, rocks and sedimentary, or deposited, rocks. The surface is called the crust. Below the crust is the mantle. This is a thick layer of heavier rocks, up to 2900 kilometres deep. Below this the rocks are molten (melted) because it is so hot. At the centre of the Earth is a core of solid rock, probably made of nickel and iron. The core acts as a giant magnet.

See also CALENDAR; FOSSIL; MOUNTAIN; OCEAN; PLANET; RIVER; ROCK; VOLCANO.

EARTHQUAKE

The Earth's crust is made up of plates of rock, which can move and break. When they do, the ground shakes causing earthquakes.

Not all earthquakes are major, destructive movements. About twenty severe earthquakes occur each year. But there are about a million minor tremors as well. Earthquakes are detected by instruments called seismometers.

See also VOLCANO.

ECHO

Sometimes when we shout, the sound of our voice comes back again a few seconds later. This is

cause an eclipse of the Sun. This happens when the Moon passes in front of the Sun and blots out the Sun's light. The Moon's shadow falls on the Earth and the sky goes dark. Then, as the Moon's shadow passes by, daylight returns. An eclipse of the Moon occurs when it moves into the shadow of the Earth.

ECOLOGY

Ecology is the study of plants and animals and how they live in their natural communities. This science shows how living things make use of their surroundings, or environment, and how they affect one another.

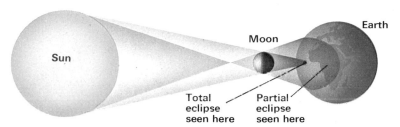

▲ **When the Moon** is directly in line between the Earth and the Sun, people in its shadow see a total eclipse of the Sun. People farther away see a partial eclipse.

an echo. It happens when the sound is reflected by an object some distance away. Bats use sound echoes to find the insects they eat. Ships and submarines use sound echoes (sonar) to detect objects under water. Airports use echoes of radio waves (radar) to track aircraft.

ECLIPSE

When one heavenly body passes in front of another and blots out its light, we say an eclipse is taking place. The Moon can

Most plants and animals can only live in a particular kind of environment such as a desert, a pond, a marsh or a forest. Each plant is suited to the temperature, soil and water supply of the ground it grows in. Animals eat the plants or other animals. This link between plants and animals is called a food web.

EDISON, Thomas A. (1847–1931)

Edison was one of the world's greatest inventors. He patented nearly 1300 inventions. Among these were the gramophone, the electric light and an electric generating station. He said he owed his success not to genius but to hard work.

See also INVENTION.

EEC

EEC stands for European Economic Community. This organization is also known as the Common Market. It is a group of countries in western Europe. There are ten members: Belgium, the Netherlands, Luxembourg, France, Greece, West Germany, Italy, Denmark, Ireland (Eire), the United Kingdom, Spain and Portugal. They work and trade together. The EEC has a civil service, a parliament and a court.

EEL

The life story of the common eel is very strange. These eels live in rivers in Europe and North America. But they migrate to the sea to breed. They make an amazing journey, swimming downstream and even wriggling overland until they reach the sea. The eels lay their eggs far out in the Atlantic Ocean. Then they die. The young eels, called elvers, swim back to the rivers. The long journey can take three years.

Some eels, such as the conger eel, spend all their lives in the sea.

▲ **Edison** is shown with two of his inventions: the electric light bulb and the gramophone.

EGG

All animal life comes from some sort of egg. Some are laid by the female and develop outside her body before they hatch. Most mammals develop inside the mother's body. The egg, or ovum, must be joined with a sperm cell before it can develop.

82

EGYPT

Modern Egypt is a country of over 48 million people. Nearly all of them live on only four per cent of the country's total area (1,002,000 square kilometres). This is the land irrigated by the Nile. The rest is desert.

Most Egyptians work on the land. They produce cotton, rice, fruits, grain and vegetables. In some areas modern irrigation has been so successful that two or three crops are grown a year.

Egypt is an independent Arab republic. The major religion is Islam and the language is Arabic.

See also page 64.

EGYPT, ANCIENT

The civilization of ancient Egypt was centred on the River Nile. The Nile valley is hot and dry, but each year the river floods and spreads a rich silt over the land, making it fertile. The ancient Egyptians worshipped the Nile as a god.

The pharaohs (kings) of Egypt were very powerful. The people thought the pharaoh was a god. He owned everything and everyone had to obey his commands. The great pharaohs built huge tombs, often in the form of pyramids. The dead pharaoh was buried inside, surrounded by treasure and by all the things he would need in the next world, such as food, clothes, furniture and weapons. The dead body was preserved, or *mummified*, before being buried. From these tombs, archaeologists have learned much about ancient Egypt.

Rich Egyptians enjoyed lives of luxury. They had servants, slaves, dancers and musicians. Ancient Egyptian civilization began around 3200 BC and lasted until 30 BC, when Egypt was finally conquered by the Romans.

▼ A wealthy household of Ancient Egypt.

E

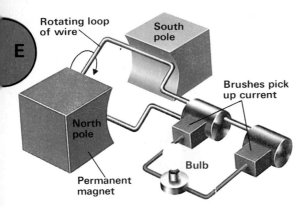

Rotating loop of wire

South pole

Brushes pick up current

North pole

Bulb

Permanent magnet

◀ **A simple generator.** An electric current can be made to flow when a loop of wire is rotated in the magnetic field between the poles of a magnet. Generators in power stations follow the same principles to make electricity for homes and factories.

EINSTEIN, Albert (1879–1955)

Einstein was one of the most brilliant thinkers of modern times. He completely changed our ideas about space, time and motion and about matter and energy. Einstein said that nothing can travel faster than light. and that mass and energy were different forms of the same thing. His ideas were set out in his famous laws of relativity.

ELECTRICITY

Electricity is a form of energy. The electricity we use in our homes is produced by generators in power stations. A battery is a portable supply of electricity.

Electricity flows through wires as electric current. It is actually a flow of electrons, the tiny particles present in all atoms. They flow easily in metals, which are called good conductors of electricity. Current can only flow if a wire makes a complete loop or circuit. Switches operate gaps in the circuit to start or stop the flow of electricity.

ELECTRONICS

Electronics is the study of the way electrons act as they flow through certain crystals, gases or a vacuum. Electrons are tiny particles found in all atoms. Electronics explains how radar and television work. Electronic devices like transistors and silicon chips are used in radios, calculators and computers.

See also COMPUTER; RADAR; RADIO; SILICON CHIP; TELEVISION; TRANSISTOR.

ELEMENTS & COMPOUNDS

Elements are the building blocks from which all substances are formed. When a chemist splits up salt, he finds that it is made up of two substances called sodium and chlorine. No matter how hard he tries, he cannot split sodium and chlorine any further. They are chemical elements. In nature there are 94 elements. And scientists have made another twelve.

Elements are made up of atoms. Groups of atoms joined

together are called molecules. For example, a molecule of oxygen consists of two oxygen atoms. A substance whose molecules contain more than one kind of atom is called a compound. Most elements are found as chemical compounds.

▲ **Today African elephants** are closely guarded against poachers who kill them for their valuable ivory tusks.

ELEPHANT

The elephant is the largest living land animal. A big male, or bull, may weigh 7 tonnes. Elephants live in herds. If one elephant is injured, the rest will help it. Elephants eat huge amounts of grass and tree leaves every day.

There are two kinds of elephant. The Indian elephant can be trained to work. But the larger African elephant is not easily tamed.

ELIZABETH I (1533–1603)

When Elizabeth was born, her father, Henry VIII, was furious. He wanted a son to succeed him as King of England. But when Elizabeth became queen in 1558, she proved a strong ruler. She never married, and for 45 years successfully protected England against its chief enemies, France and Spain. Daring seamen, such as Francis Drake, and brilliant writers, like William Shakespeare, made her reign one of the most exciting in English history.

EMU

The emu is an Australian bird, almost as large as an ostrich. It cannot fly, but can run swiftly. It has long brown feathers which look more like hairs. Emus eat mainly roots and plants.

ENERGY

When a piece of wood is set alight, it burns and gives out light you can see and heat you can feel. Heat and light are two common forms of energy.

Wood is one kind of fuel, which releases energy when it is burnt. Coal, petrol and natural gas are other fuels. When petrol is burned in a car engine, the energy produced makes pistons turn the car wheels.

The *chemical energy* in the fuel has been changed into *mechanical energy* to turn the car wheels. When the car is moving it has *kinetic energy*, the energy of motion. A rock balancing on top of a cliff has *potential energy* – the energy of position.

ENGINE

We use many kinds of engines in the modern world to work the machines in our homes and factories, and those which transport us in the air and on the roads. Most engines burn a fuel to produce energy to move the machine parts. A car engine burns petrol, while lorries and buses have diesel engines, which burn oil. Aircraft have jet engines, which burn kerosene (paraffin). There are all kinds of internal combustion engines, in which fuel is burned in an enclosed space. Steam engines and turbines burn fuel outside the engine.

See also ENERGY; FUEL; JET ENGINE.

86

▶**Europe** is a continent of contrasts – from cold frozen tundra and pine forests in the north, to the sun-parched plains of the south. There are lush green valleys and snow-capped mountains, open farmlands and crowded cities. Europe is a centre of art and learning. Its many famous buildings show some of the continent's fascinating history.

BRITISH ISLES

FRANC

Atlantic Ocean

The Pyrenees

PORTUGAL   SPAIN

AFRICA

ESKIMO

The Eskimos live in the cold Arctic regions. All Eskimos once hunted for their food. They travelled in skin canoes, called kayaks, and on sledges. In summer they lived in skin tents and in

Arctic Ocean

SCANDINAVIA

North Sea

Baltic Sea

USSR

EASTERN EUROPE

GERMANY

The Alps

AUSTRIA

Black Sea

ITALY

ASIA

Mediterranean Sea

GREECE

winter they built igloos. Most Eskimos now live in modern settlements.

EUROPE

The continent of Europe is smaller than any of the other continents except Australia. Yet a fifth of the world's people live in Europe.

Most of Europe has fertile soil and good rainfall. Europe's farmers produce meat, grain, fruit and vegetables. Most farms use

87

modern machinery. Europe is rich in coal, iron ore and other raw materials.

Europe lives by trade. It has good roads, railways, airports and canals. Ships carry goods across the Baltic Sea, the North Sea and the Mediterranean Sea, and to all parts of the world.

The people of Europe are made up of many different nationalities. Each has its own language and customs. In the past, European countries have fought with each other. European wars affected the rest of the world, because European countries were so powerful. Two world wars in this century have begun in Europe.

Today, the European countries are among the richest in the world. They try to live peacefully together. But there are divisions still. Most of the countries of eastern Europe have communist governments while the western countries are democracies.

See also page 64.

EVOLUTION

Evolution is the gradual process by which all living things have changed since life began millions of years ago. Fossils show us how creatures have changed.

The first creatures were very simple forms of life. They evolved into more complicated plants and animals. Fishes evolved from smaller sea creatures. Some fish began breathing air and crawled on to dry land. These were the first amphibians. The amphibians evolved into reptiles. All birds and mammals, including man, evolved from reptiles.

EXPLORERS

People have always had the urge to explore the unknown. Some explorers have gone in search of lands to settle. Others were greedy for riches, while some

▼ **Roald Amundsen** was the first to reach the South Pole in 1911.

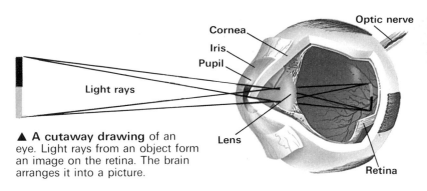

▲ **A cutaway drawing** of an eye. Light rays from an object form an image on the retina. The brain arranges it into a picture.

journeyed only in search of knowledge.

To the ancient peoples of Europe, 'the world' meant the lands around the Mediterranean Sea. Only the Phoenicians dared sail out into the grey Atlantic Ocean beyond.

In the 900s the Vikings sailed in their small, fragile ships as far as North America. But until the invention of the magnetic compass in the 1300s, long sea voyages were very dangerous.

To reach the East, with its gold, spices and silks, European merchants had to travel overland. Marco Polo reached China in 1275. Then the Portuguese discovered they could arrive at India by sailing round the coast of Africa. In 1492 Columbus reached America, the 'New World'. By 1522 Magellan's sailors had proved that the world was round by sailing round it.

After this explorers went out from Europe eager to finds lands to settle as colonies. The last continent to be explored by Europeans was Africa. During the 1800s several explorers crossed this unknown continent. Then in 1909 Peary reached the North Pole, and in 1911 Amundsen beat Scott to the South Pole. Today few parts of the Earth are unexplored.

See also COLUMBUS; COOK; DA GAMA; MAGELLAN; MARCO POLO; VIKINGS.

EYE

Our eyes are very delicate. Each eye is a ball full of liquid. In the centre of the front is a black hole called the *pupil*. This lets in light. Behind the pupil is a *lens*. The lens focuses an image of whatever we are looking at on to a screen called the *retina*. Then messages are sent along a nerve to the brain. The brain arranges the messages into a picture again, and we 'see'.

The coloured part of the eye is called the *iris*. It is a ring of muscle which makes the pupil larger or smaller. In bright light, the pupil gets smaller. But in dim light, it gets larger to let in as much light as possible.

were better ploughs, seed drills, threshers and reapers, and tractors replaced the horse and ox. Discoveries about crop rotation fertilizers and chemicals allowed farmers to grow larger crops.

▼ **Huge wheat farms** are found on the temperate grasslands of North America.

FARMING

Farming is the world's most important industry. By raising animals and growing crops, farmers provide us with food. Civilization became possible only when people stopped being nomadic and settled down to farm.

Gradually, people learned how to plant seeds and grow crops, and how to keep and breed animals such as chickens, cattle and sheep. Slowly, tools were devised to help.

In the 1800s and 1900s machines were invented to do the work of people and animals. There

FERN

Ferns are primitive plants. There have been ferns on Earth for over 300 million years. Some prehistoric ferns were as tall as trees.

Ferns have no flowers or seeds. Instead they have tiny cells called spores under their leaves. The wind scatters the spores on to the ground and they grow into tiny plants. Later these plants grow into new ferns.

FERTILIZER

A fertilizer is a substance that contains food which plants need. Plants use about twelve different foods from the soil. They need

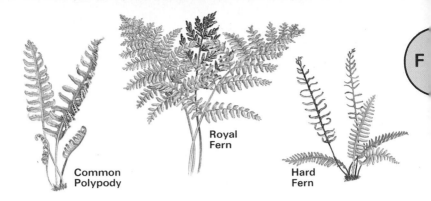

Common Polypody

Royal Fern

Hard Fern

some, such as nitrogen, phosphorus and potassium, in greater amounts than are usually found in the soil. So fertilizers are added to their soil.

Some fertilizers are made from natural substances; others are mainly chemicals.

FILM

'Moving pictures' were first shown in the 1890s. People crowded into cinemas to watch them. During the 1930s, because of its good weather and varied scenery, Hollywood in the USA, became the centre of the film industry. At first films were silent and rather jerky. 'Talking pictures' appeared in 1927.

The person who decides how a story is made into a film is the director. The producer takes care of the business side. And, apart from the actors and cameramen, there are people to look after scenery, lighting, costumes, makeup and 'stunts'. Sometimes a studio set, with artificial scenery, is used. But films are often 'shot' (filmed) out of doors 'on

location'. When filming is over, the best parts of the film are edited (cut up and run together) to make the finished film.

▲ **Some standard** fingerprint patterns.

FINGERPRINTS

The tiny ridges and furrows arranged in patterns on the tips of the fingers and thumbs are called fingerprints. No two people have the same fingerprints. Even if the outer skin is damaged the pattern does not change. This is why fingerprints are so helpful to the police in identifying criminals.

91

FISH

Fishes are animals which spend their lives in water. Some fishes live in salt water and some live in fresh water. Some spend part of their lives in the sea, and part in the rivers.

Most fishes have bony skeletons. But a small group including sharks have skeletons made of gristle, or cartilage. Like all animals, fishes have to breathe oxygen. Their gills take oxygen out of the water. Some fishes breathe through their skins as well, and a few have lungs.

Fishes eat water animals, including other fishes, and plants. They swim by bending their bodies from side to side, and by moving their tails. They use their fins to keep them upright and for steering and braking.

Most fishes are covered with scales. Some fishes have a line of special scales along each side of

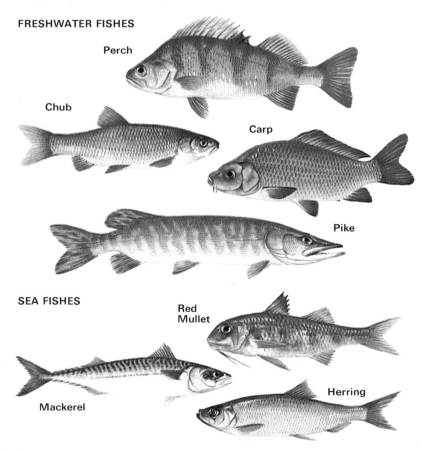

FRESHWATER FISHES

Perch

Chub

Carp

Pike

SEA FISHES

Red Mullet

Mackerel

Herring

the body. This is called the lateral line. It helps the fish detect underwater vibrations. Most fishes have an air bladder inside their bodies to keep them at any level they choose. But the more primitive cartilage fishes do not have this 'swim bladder'. If they stop swimming they sink.

During the breeding season some fishes migrate over long distances to reach their spawning grounds. Most fishes lay their eggs and leave them floating in the water. Out of millions of eggs, only a few survive. Other fishes lay fewer eggs, but take more care of them.

See also EEL; SEAHORSE; SHARK.

▼ **Some of the nets** and a trap used in sea fishing.

FISHING

Most fish are caught in the sea; but in some countries river and lake fisheries are important. The best fishing grounds are in the Atlantic and Pacific oceans.

The most important food fish are cod, mackerel, haddock, herring, flatfish (such as plaice and sole), sardine, tunny (or tuna) and salmon. Shellfish, such as prawns, lobsters and oysters, also make valuable catches.

Most sea fish are caught in nets. *Trawls* are long, bag-shaped nets towed along under water. A *purse-seine* net is drawn round a shoal of fish, then pulled up. *Gill nets* look rather like curtains: the fish swim into them and are caught in the mesh. Fish can also be caught on baited lines. This method is known as *lining* or *trolling*.

F

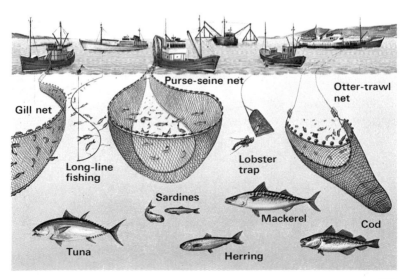

Gill net

Purse-seine net

Otter-trawl net

Long-line fishing

Lobster trap

Sardines

Mackerel

Cod

Tuna

Herring

FLAGS

1. Albania	37. N. Korea
2. Algeria	38. S. Korea
3. Argentina	39. Lebanon
4. Australia	40. Liberia
5. Austria	41. Malaysia
6. Belgium	42. Malta
7. Bolivia	43. Mexico
8. Brazil	44. Morocco
9. Bulgaria	45. Netherlands
10. Burma	46. New Zealand
11. Canada	47. Nigeria
12. Sri Lanka	48. Norway
13. Chile	49. Pakistan
14. China	50. Peru
15. Colombia	51. Philippines
16. Cuba	52. Poland
17. Czechoslovakia	53. Portugal
18. Denmark	54. Romania
19. Ecuador	55. Saudi Arabia
20. Ethiopia	56. Sierra Leone
21. Finland	57. Singapore
22. France	58. South Africa
23. E. Germany	59. Spain
24. W. Germany	60. Sweden
25. Ghana	61. Switzerland
26. Greece	62. Thailand
27. Hungary	63. Trinidad & Tobago
28. Iceland	64. Tunisia
29. India	65. Turkey
30. Indonesia	66. United Kingdom
31. Iraq	67. USA
32. Ireland	68. Uruguay
33. Israel	69. USSR
34. Italy	70. Venezuela
35. Jamaica	71. Yugoslavia
36. Japan	72. Zaire

FLAG

Every country has its own flag. Organizations such as the United Nations and the Red Cross have flags, and kings and queens have their own personal flags.

The first flags were ornamental streamers. In battle, flags or standards, raised high on poles, were rallying points for soldiers.

In the Middle Ages there were several flags of different shapes, (gonfalons, banners and pennons) but today most are rectangular. Flags are also used at sea to identify ships and to send messages.

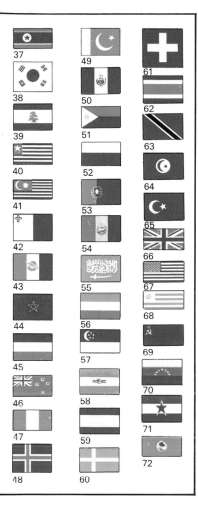

FLEA

The flea is a small, wingless insect. It has three pairs of strong legs that are especially good for jumping. It lives on and sucks the blood of birds and animals including humans. Fleas can be dangerous because they move among animals carrying diseases.

FLOWER

Most plants have flowers. The flower is the part of the plant where the seeds develop. Without it, the plant could not reproduce itself. Inside each seed is all the 'information' needed to make a new plant grow. Most flowers appear in the summer when the plant is fully grown. Flowers come in all shapes and sizes, but they all have the same basic parts.

The most important parts are called *stamens* and *carpels*. The stamens are male parts, which produce a powder called *pollen*. The carpels are female parts. Each carpel has a sticky top, called a *stigma*. It is sticky so that pollen will cling to it. When this happens, the *ovule* in the lower part of the carpel can develop into a seed.

See also FRUIT; PLANT.

▼ **This diagram** shows the parts of a typical flower. Some flowers have only one ovule. Others have hundreds. After they are fertilized, ovules develop into seeds.

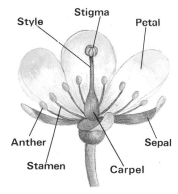

95

FLY

There are more than 750,000 different kinds of flies – one of the largest groups of insects in the world. Flies have only one pair of wings.

Some flies are harmless but many carry germs and spread dangerous diseases. For instance, a housefly will land on a piece of human food and vomit up a drop of its own last meal. It sucks up most of it but millions of bacteria remain behind in an infectious fly speck.

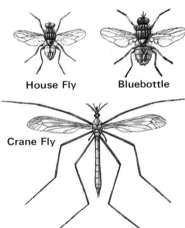

House Fly   Bluebottle

Crane Fly

FOG

A cloud that forms close to the ground is called fog. Fog is formed when warm, moist air passes over cool land or water, or when cool air comes down over warm water or moist land. The water vapour in the air turns into tiny drops of water. That is why fog feels damp. After a clear warm day, heat from the land may cause a thin fog to form.

FOOD

Our bodies need energy to live and grow. This energy comes from the food we eat. The three most important substances in food are *carbohydrates, fats* and *proteins.* Carbohydrates are food 'fuels'. They give us energy to work, move and keep warm, Sugar and starch are carbohydrates. We eat carbohydrates in bread, potatoes, rice, sweets and cakes. Cream, butter and the fat in meat provide us with fats. These are also good fuels. But if we eat too many carbohydrates or fats, our bodies store what they cannot use. Then we get fat. Proteins build the body's cells and are vital to good health. Protein-rich foods are eggs, lean meat, cheese, fish and beans.

▼ **A dramatic leap** during the final match for the soccer World Cup, 1982, between Italy and Germany. Italy won the cup.

FOOTBALL
There are seven different games of football: Australian Rugby, Canadian, American, Gaelic, Rugby League, Rugby Union and Association (or Soccer). They all come from a rough game played in England as long ago as the Middle Ages. Any number of players took part and there were no rules.

Soccer is now the only kind of football in which handling the ball is not allowed.

FORD, Henry (1863–1947)
Henry Ford was an American automobile manufacturer. He was the first man to develop assembly-line methods of production. In mass-production the parts of the car are added to the car body on a conveyor belt. Ford could produce many cars very cheaply. Between 1908 and 1927 he mass-produced 15 million Model T cars alone.

FOREST
Land that is covered with trees is forest. Today about a third of the Earth's land surface is covered by forests. There are about 20,000 different kinds of tree, and about 1000 of them produce good timber.

In cold lands the forests are mainly of conifers, such as pines and firs. The largest coniferous forests are in northern Europe, Canada and Siberia.

Milder countries have forests of broad-leaved trees, such as oaks, elms, beeches, birches and maples. These trees are deciduous, that is, they shed their leaves every year.

In the hot, wet lands close to the Equator there are tropical forests of trees such as ebony and mahogany, whose wood is very hard. There are vast rain forests in South America, central Africa and southeast Asia. Near the coasts, are often found swamp forests of mangroves.

▲ **This fossil** of the *Eoplatax* fish is about 50 million years old.

FOSSIL
Fossils are the hardened remains of dead animals and plants that lived thousands of years ago. They tell us what life was like before written records were kept.

Some fossils are the impressions made by remains which have since disappeared. They are often found in rock because the plants and animals were covered by mud or sand which later turned into rock.

Sometimes a whole body is preserved including the hair and skin. Sometimes the body has dissolved away and the space it left filled with mud or sand that slowly turned into rock. Most commonly, though, fossils are just the remains of the hard parts of animals such as bones or shells.

FOX

Foxes belong to the dog family. They hunt by night for rabbits, mice and voles. The female fox is called a vixen. She rears her cubs in an underground den.

Red Fox

Farmers dislike foxes, because they raid hen houses. In Britain the fox is hunted by foxhounds. Silver and blue Arctic foxes are bred on special farms for their fur. The little fennec fox lives in the desert.

FRANCE

France is the largest country in western Europe. Its beautiful scenery includes forests, plains, valleys, high mountains and great rivers.

France has fertile soil and a mild climate. Many of its people are farmers. Throughout France grapes are grown to make wine, French cheeses are also famous. France has many industries and is a member of the EEC. Its capital city is Paris.

In 1789 the French people overthrew their king and set up a republic. This important event is called the French Revolution.

▲ **Thousands of people** visit Paris, the French capital, each year. In the background is the Arc de Triomphe.

See also page 64.

FROGS AND TOADS

These animals are amphibians. They can live on land, but must return to the water to lay eggs.

Frogs and toads look rather alike. But frogs use their long back legs to hop. Toads crawl or run. Both eat insects and worms, catching their prey with their long, sticky tongues.

In spring frogs and toads travel to ponds and streams to breed. They lay eggs called spawn. The eggs hatch into tadpoles. Tadpoles swim like fish and breathe through gills. But soon they grow legs, lose their tails and develop lungs. Finally, they become tiny frogs or toads.

plants can grow. Some fruits have wings (such as the sycamore) or light, fluffy heads (such as the dandelion) so that the seeds will blow away. Other fruits are sweet and juicy, so that animals will carry them away as food. Burrs are fruits which cling to the fur of passing animals. Many fruits split when ripe, letting their seeds fall.

See also FLOWER; PLANT.

▼ **The life cycle** of the frog. The eggs or spawn grow into a tadpole. Tadpoles breathe like fish through gills. As they grow they develop legs and their gills become lungs. After three months they become baby frogs.

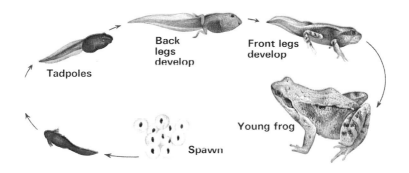

Tadpoles

Back legs develop

Front legs develop

Young frog

Spawn

FRUIT

We all recognize apples, bananas and oranges as fruits. But pea pods, walnuts, cucumbers, acorns and dandelion 'clocks' are also fruits. Many fruits are good to eat and growing them is an important industry.

The fruit is the part of a plant which protects the seed. It helps to spread the seed, so that new

FUEL

Fuels are substances that release energy when burnt. The process of burning is called combustion.

Fuel may be solid, liquid or gas. Coal, wood, charcoal and peat are solid fuels. The most important liquid fuels come from petroleum. Natural gas, a compound of hydrogen and carbon, is often found near petroleum.

G

GALAXY

Our Sun is part of a great family of stars. We call this family the Milky Way galaxy, or just the Galaxy. A galaxy is a big group of stars which move together through space. Each galaxy contains about 100,000 million stars and probably many planets. Some stars are grouped together in giant *clusters*. The galaxies also contain great clouds of gas and dust called *nebulae*.

▼ **The Andromeda Galaxy** is very like our own Galaxy.

GALILEO (1564–1642)

Galileo was an Italian astronomer. In 1609 he became the first person to look at the sky through a telescope. He saw the mountains on our Moon and the moons of the planet Jupiter.

Galileo was skilled at mathematics and carried out scientific experiments. He discovered how a pendulum swings and showed that different weights fall to the ground at the same rate.

GAMA, Vasco da (c1460–1524)

This Portuguese explorer was the first man to find a sea route to India. He sailed from Lisbon in July 1497, rounded the Cape of Good Hope in November and went on to land in south-western India in May 1498. He returned to Portugal with two ships laden with spices.

GANDHI, Mohandas Karamchand (1869–1948)

Gandhi helped to free India from British rule. Known as the Mahatma or 'Great Soul', he believed that all violence was wrong. So he used 'peaceful non-cooperation' as a weapon against his opponents. He was born in India. From 1893 to 1915 he worked against racial hatred in South Africa.

When India became independent in 1947, Muslims and Hindus began fighting. Gandhi failed to make peace between them, and was shot by a Hindu fanatic on January 30th, 1948.

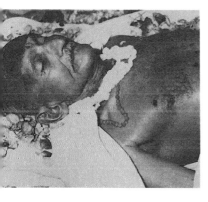

GARIBALDI, Giuseppe (1807–1882)

Garibaldi was an Italian patriot. In his time Italy was made up of several separate states and large parts of northern Italy belonged to Austria. Garibaldi fought to make Italy one country from 1834 until 1860. Then Victor Emmanuel became king of the whole of Italy.

▲ **Galileo** with the telescope with which he discovered the moons of Jupiter.

◄ **Gandhi** lying in state after his assassination in 1948. Vast crowds came to mourn at his funeral.

GAS

All the substances that make up our world can exist in three forms – as a solid, liquid or gas. Gases are different from the other two forms because they have no shape and completely fill anything they are put in.

The air we breathe is a gas, or rather a mixture of gases. It contains mainly oxygen and nitrogen. All living things need oxygen to live. We breathe in oxygen and breathe out another gas – carbon dioxide.

Some gases, such as natural gas and hydrogen, are valuable as fuels. Others like chlorine, carbon monoxide and hydrogen sulphide are very poisonous.
See also FUEL; OXYGEN.

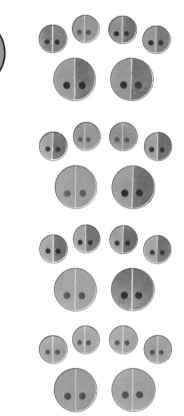

◀ **Genetic patterns.** If both parents have two blue eye genes, all their children will have blue eyes. If one parent has two brown eye genes and the other has two blue eye genes, the children will all have brown eyes because the brown gene is dominant. But those children will have what is called a recessive blue eye gene. If they have children with a blue-eyed person, or another person with a recessive blue gene, some of their children may have blue eyes.

GENETICS

The science of genetics explains why living things look and behave as they do. Advanced animals have two sexes, male and female. Each individual produces sex cells. If a male and female sex cell join, the female cell grows into a new individual. Each parent passes on certain characteristics to its offspring. This process is called *heredity*.

Heredity works in an amazing way. Inside every cell are tiny *chromosomes*, largely made of a chemical called DNA. Different parts of each chromosome carry different 'coded messages'. Each part is called a *gene*. The genes carry all the information needed to make a new plant or animal. They decide its sex and also what characteristics it inherits.

Some inherited characteristics are stronger than others. They are 'dominant'. Weaker ones are 'recessive'. Genes for brown eyes, for example, dominate over the weaker genes for blue eyes.

GEM

Some rocks contain beautiful crystals that can be cut to show great brilliance and sparkle. They are called gems or gemstones. They can be set in gold, platinum and silver to form beautiful pieces of jewellery.

The finest gems are diamonds. Red rubies, green emeralds and blue sapphires are also valuable. Some gems are not crystals, but lovely stones. They include opal and lapis lazuli. Pearls are gems that oysters produce in their shells.

▲ **Polished opals** photographed in front of the rock or ore in which they are found.

▲ **The Mosel Valley** in West Germany is a famous wine-producing region.

GENGHIS KHAN (1167–1227) Genghis Khan was one of the most feared men in history. He was born Temujin, son of a Mongol prince, but became known as Genghis Khan, meaning 'conqueror of the world'. The Mongols came from central Asia. Wherever Genghis Khan led his Mongol army, terrible tales were told of his cruelty. He conquered many tribes in China, Russia, Afghanistan and Persia and so won an enormous empire for the Mongols.

GERMANY
Two countries in Europe are called Germany. Until 1945 each was part of a single country, called Germany. Germany began two devastating wars in this century – World War I (1914–18) and World War II (1939–45). After World War II the Russians controlled the eastern part (now East Germany or the DDR), while the western allies held the rest (West Germany). Berlin, the old capital, was also divided.

Only northern Germany has a sea coast on the North and Baltic Seas. Here the land is mostly flat. Central Germany is hilly and wooded, and in the south are high mountains and thick forests.

Germany has fertile soil and a mild climate. Farmers grow cereals, potatoes and sugar beet, and make grapes into wine. They raise cattle and pigs.

Germany has plenty of coal, iron ore, timber and hydro-electric power. So industry is important. There are many factories, especially in the Ruhr in West Germany.

Both Germanies have built up new, modern industries. West Germany is a member of the EEC. East Germany is not so rich and the people have less freedom. See also page 64.

GEYSER

A geyser is a spring which spouts hot water and steam into the air from time to time. It is a small sign of the searing heat deep inside the Earth.

A geyser consists of a hole which goes down to a layer of hot rock (usually uncooled lava) and water. When the water is superheated by the rocks it erupts or shoots into the air.

Geysers are found in many volcanic regions. The most famous are in Japan, in the USA and in New Zealand.

See also VOLCANO

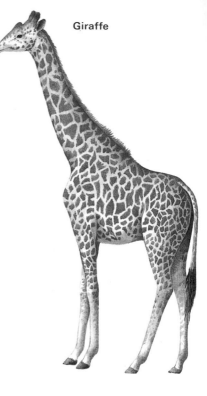

Giraffe

GIRAFFE

The giraffe is the tallest animal in the world. It may reach nearly 6 metres in height. Giraffes live in Africa. They eat leaves, not grass, and when they drink, they have to spread their legs wide in order to reach the water. They run swiftly to escape their enemies.

◀ **The Diamond Geyser,** Rotorua, New Zealand, erupts to over nine metres.

104

▶ **A glacier** in the Swiss Alps.

GLACIER

A glacier is a slow-moving river of ice. It flows down the slopes of mountains from an icecap or high snow field. Glaciers push stones and boulders along with them. They scrape the soil from the land, smooth the hills and scour out valleys. The rocky mounds piled up by glaciers are called *moraines*.

During the Ice Ages glaciers spread across the northern hemisphere. Boulders carried with the ice can still be seen, even though the glaciers melted long ago.
See also ICE AGE; ICEBERG.

GLASS

Glass is a useful material. It is transparent, easy to shape, and cheap to make. It can be made as flat sheets for windows, or into curved lenses for cameras, microscopes and other instruments. It can be blown to make bottles, tumblers and other objects.

Glass is made from some of the cheapest materials you can think of – sand, limestone and soda ash. These three ingredients are mixed together and heated in a very hot furnace. They melt and become glass.

GOAT

The goat was one of the earliest animals to be tamed. Its milk, meat, wool and skin have been useful to people for thousands of years.

The goat is tougher than its relative the sheep. It can live in dry, rocky country. It climbs well and can eat almost anything. Herds of hungry goats have turned good pastures into deserts. Wild goats live on high mountain crags.

Goat

GOLD

Gold is a heavy, yellow metal. It has been used for thousands of years to make jewellery and ornaments because it is beautiful and does not lose its shine. It is also easy to shape. It can be

105

drawn into fine wire or beaten into thin sheets without snapping. Gold is precious because it is scarce. It is found in the ground as a metal. Sometimes large lumps of gold, or nuggets, are mined in the rocks. But usually gold is found in lodes or veins in rocks. Half the world's gold is mined in just one part of South Africa.

See also METAL.

▲ **Gold bars** stacked in a vault.

GOVERNMENT

Government was needed as soon as people began living in groups. People living together in a group have to agree on what jobs must be done and who should do them. In a primitive tribe the best hunter or strongest warrior might become the ruler or chief.

The ancient Greeks were the first to try a form of government called *democracy* or 'rule by the people'. The people met to discuss new laws and to decide what taxes should be paid. This was the beginning of the modern *parliament*.

Today every country has a head of state. Britain is a monarchy, so the head of state is the Queen. But the country is ruled by a government of ministers. The head of the government is the Prime Minister. Parliament is divided into two parts, the House of Commons and the House of Lords.

In the United States the President is head of state and head of the government. He also commands the armed forces. Presidents are elected every four years. The US parliament, called the Congress, is divided into the House of Representatives and the Senate.

In a democracy more than one political party is allowed. But in Communist countries, only the Communist Party takes part in the government.

See also COMMUNISM; DEMOCRACY.

GRASS

Most grasses are slender, with hollow stems and pointed leaves. The plants keep growing even when the leaves are cut.

Cereals are grasses that are also valuable foods. Many farm animals eat grass, fresh in summer and dried as hay in winter. Sugar cane is a kind of grass.

▶ **A mountain grasshopper.** Grasshoppers spend most of their time in long grass.

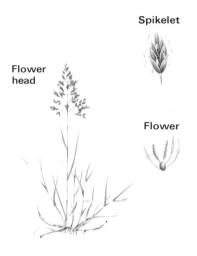

Spikelet

Flower head

Flower

▲ **Grasses** have thin, wiry roots. The flowers are arranged in groups called spikelets.

GRASSHOPPER

Grasshoppers are insects. They live in fields and meadows and feed on green plants. They can hop as much as 75 centimetres. The male grasshopper chirps to attract a mate. He does this by rubbing the insides of his back legs against his wings.

GRAVITY

Throw a ball into the air and it will fall back to the ground. This is because the Earth pulls it back. The Earth's pull is called gravity. Gravity is one of the basic forces in the Universe. Magnetism is another. Isaac Newton first stated the laws of gravity. He said that every object in the universe has an attraction for every other object.

Gravity is what keeps all the heavenly bodies in their paths through the heavens. It keeps the Moon moving in a circle around the Earth. It keeps the Earth moving around the Sun. If there were no gravity, the Moon and Earth would fly off into space.

GREECE, ANCIENT

The ancient Greeks built one of the greatest of all civilizations. It began some 4000 years ago when wandering tribes from central Europe came to the land that we now call Greece.

Over the centuries, the Greek civilization developed. Cities were built. Craftsmen made beautiful gold ornaments and bronze weapons. Art, music and poetry developed.

About 2500 years ago the Greeks of Athens set up a new form of government, called *democracy*, which means 'rule by the people'. All the citizens had a right to say how they were to be ruled. This was an important new idea.

Life in Athens was relaxed. The Athenians built fine temples and public buildings. For entertainment, the Athenians played music on flutes and lyres or they went to the theatre. The Athenians loved to hear stories of great Greek heroes and their deeds. The greatest of these stories were told by the poet Homer in two long poems, called the *Iliad* and the *Odyssey*. The beauty of life in Athens can be seen from the ruins which still remain.

Athens was only one of a number of city states in Greece. The states often quarrelled. The greatest rival of Athens was Sparta, and the two states were very different. Sparta was a military state, ruled by all-powerful kings. Its people were soldiers and the Spartans had no use for art, philosophy or comfortable homes.

The Greeks were very fond of athletics, such as running, javelin and discus throwing and wrestling. The first Olympic Games, named after Mount Olympus, home of the Greek gods, took place in 776 BC. The Greeks had many gods, but the greatest was Zeus, king of the gods.

The age of the city states ended in Greece in 338 BC. Then, King Philip of Macedonia brought all of Greece under his rule.

Greek ideas have survived many centuries, and have had great influence. The way we live and think today owes a great deal to the civilization of ancient Greece.

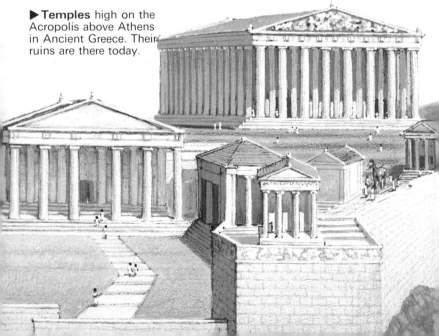

▶**Temples** high on the Acropolis above Athens in Ancient Greece. Their ruins are there today.

Guinea-pig

Hamster

tor and drifts past Florida up the coast of the United States towards Newfoundland and then moves towards Europe.

Part of the Gulf Stream washes the shores of France, the British Isles, Norway and Iceland. Because it is warm, winter in these countries is much milder than that of other places just as far north.

G

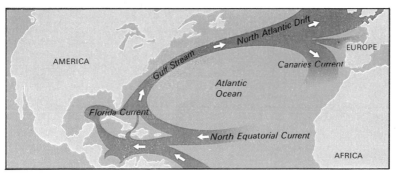

AMERICA

Gulf Stream

North Atlantic Drift

EUROPE

Canaries Current

Atlantic Ocean

Florida Current

←North Equatorial Current

AFRICA

GUINEA-PIG

The guinea-pig is a member of the rodent family. Guinea-pigs have four toes on their front feet and three on their hind feet.

All varieties of guinea-pig are descended from the wild cavy of the Andes. Long before Europeans went to America, the Indians there had tamed it and kept it for its meat.

GULF STREAM

The Gulf Stream is a very important warm-water ocean current. It is surface water which flows in a clockwise movement around the north Atlantic Ocean. It begins near the Equa-

GUN

Guns are weapons which fire bullets or shells. Small arms, also called firearms, include pistols, revolvers, shotguns, and rifles. Big military guns – artillery pieces – include field guns howitzers and mortars.

All guns work in roughly the same way. A gun has a long, hollow, metal *barrel*. The *bore* of a gun is the width of the hole in the barrel. One end of the barrel, the *breech*, is closed; the other end, the *muzzle*, is open. When the gun is fired, an explosive charge inside a *cartridge* sends a bullet down the barrel and out of the muzzle with great force.

GUTENBERG, Johannes (c1398–1468)

Gutenberg invented movable type for printing in about 1439. His invention meant that books could be produced cheaply. Knowledge, once available only to a few people, could now be studied by many.

GYMNASTICS

Gymnastics consists of exercises which develop and strengthen the body. There are two main types of gymnastics – Swedish and German. They were developed in the early 19th century. Both these systems help make people supple, strong, graceful and agile. Gymnasts use apparatus such as beams, rings and horizontal and parallel bars.

Gymnastics forms part of the Olympic Games. Mastery of this sport calls for strength, artistic feeling and technical skill.

▼ **A gymnast** requires both strength and grace.

HANDEL, George Frederick (1685–1759)

Handel was a German-born English composer who was famous for his operas, concertos and oratorios. His best known works are *The Messiah*, *Fire works Music* and *Water Music*.

HANNIBAL (247–183 BC)

Hannibal, a general and statesman, was one of ancient Rome's greatest enemies. He came from Carthage in North Africa. In 218 BC he invaded Italy by crossing the Alps with his entire army including war elephants. He fought the Romans for fifteen years but was never able to crush them.

HARVEY, William (1578–1657)

Harvey was an English physician who showed how the heart functioned and proved that the blood goes round the body in a circular motion.

HEART

Your heart beats about 70 times every minute. It is a pump – a bag of extra strong muscle that pumps blood around the body.

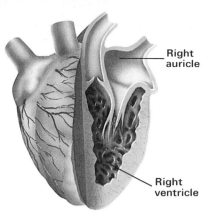

Right
auricle

Right
ventricle

▲ **A diagram** of the heart.

▲ **A helicopter** landing on an aircraft carrier.

The pump is divided into four parts: a left and right auricle above a left and right *ventricle*. The two sides of the pump work quite independently. Blood fresh from the lungs enters the left auricle and is forced through a valve down to the left ventricle. From there it is forced into the body's main artery, the aorta, and out of the heart ready to flow around the body.

On the other side, 'stale' blood from the body enters the right auricle, passes into the right ventricle and is forced out towards the lungs where it will dump its carbon dioxide and pick up vital oxygen.

HEDGEHOG
The hedgehog is one of a group of mammals called insectivores. Although the word means it eats insects, the hedgehog will eat almost anything. It rolls itself into a prickly ball when frightened and hibernates in winter.

HELICOPTER
A helicopter is a machine that can fly forwards, upwards, downwards, and sideways. This is because it has a rotor, or rotating (turning), wing. Ordinary aircraft have fixed wings and their engines can drive them forwards only. The helicopter's rotor consists of metal blades mounted on top of the body. Turned by the engine, the rotor screws itself into the air to lift the helicopter off the ground. When flying forwards, the rotor blades are angled so that they push the air backwards.

HERALDRY

Heraldry is the study of coats of arms, and the people who control and design them are known as heralds. Heraldry began during the Middle Ages. It was difficult to tell if a knight in armour was a friend or an enemy, so knights put *crests* on their helmets and painted designs called *devices* on their shields.

Each knight had his own coat of arms, which became his family badge or emblem.

HIBERNATION

In winter when food is scarce, many animals go into a long deep sleep. This is called hibernation.

During late summer and autumn, while food is still plentiful, the animal eats until its body is fat. Then it digs itself into the ground or finds a sheltered place to sleep. While the animal is asleep, its heartbeat and its breathing slows. It uses so little energy that it can live solely on the fat in its body.

◄ **These hibernating** animals all live in North America.

Butterflies

Dormouse

Woodchuck

American badger

Frog

112

HIEROGLYPHIC

This was a system of writing used in ancient Egypt. Hieroglyphics began before 3000 BC with a very simple kind of picture writing in which each picture stood for an object. Later, pictures came to represent ideas. Finally, pictures were used to represent sounds in the spoken language.

Hieroglyphics fell into disuse and remained unread until a Frenchman called Champollion deciphered inscriptions on a stone slab, the Rosetta Stone, in 1822.

HIPPOPOTAMUS

The huge hippopotamus lives in the rivers of Africa. Its name means 'river horse' but it is actually related to the pig.

Despite their gaping jaws and tusks, hippos eat only plants. They spend the day in the water, floating or walking along the river bottom, and come ashore at night. They love to wallow in mud. Hippos can be dangerous if annoyed.

▼ **A mother hippo** splashing about with her young.

HINDUS

Hinduism is a religion. Hindus believe that God is present in all things. Their most important holy books are the *Vedas*. Hindu priests or Brahmins worship the supreme God. Ordinary people worship lesser gods, such as Vishnu, God of Life.

HISTORY

History is the story of the past. Historians are mostly interested in famous people and great events, because these things affect nations. But history is also concerned with people's lives.

Science, medicine, art, religion and architecture all have histories of their own. History is revealed in many ways: by digging for it, by reading about it in old books and manuscripts and by listening to people talking.

See the history chart on pages 114–117.

BC	AFRICA
c.8000	Farming begins
c.4000–3500	Wheel, plough and sail in Egypt
c.3500	Early writing in Egypt
c.2700–c.2200	Age of Pyramids in Egypt
2050–1800	Middle Kingdom under Theban rulers
670	Assyrians conquer Egypt
525	Persians conquer Egypt
500	Nok civilization founded
332	Alexander the Great conquers Egypt
306	Ptolemy I founds new dynasty in Egypt
30	Death of Antony and Cleopatra. Rome conquers Egypt

AD	
100	Kingdom of Ethiopia founded
429–44	Vandals occupy North Africa
533–4	Belisarius reconquers North Africa for Justinian
800s	Civilization of Ghana
969	Fatimids conquer Egypt

	ASIA
c.6000	Rice cultivation in Far East
c.4000	Farming, plough, wheel in Mesopotamia
c.3000	Civilization of Sumeria
c.2700–1750	Harappan civilization in Indus Valley
c.2000–c.1200	Hittite civilization in Turkey
c.1750–1000	Shang dynasty in China
c.1200–650	Domination of Assyrian Empire
1000–c.500	Chou dynasty in China
551	Birth of Confucius
c.550–330	Achaemenid Empire in Persia
530s	Buddha preaching
334–323	Campaigns of Alexander the Great
c.320	Mauryan Empire in India
c.200BC–c.AD220	Han dynasty in China
c.6	Birth of Jesus
c.30	Crucifixion of Jesus, founder of Christianity
226–636	Sassanid Empire in Persia
304–8	Huns invade China
c.320	Gupta Empire in Ganges Valley: 'Golden Age' of Hindu culture
c.300–500	Main spread of Buddhism in China
c.520	Decimal system invented in India
540	Persian-Byzantine War begins
618–906	T'ang dynasty in China
622	Muhammad founds religion of Islam
636–750	Arabs conquer an empire from Spain to the Indus Valley
794	Japanese capital moves to Kyoto
?960–1280	Sung dynasty in China
1096	First Crusade
1192	Yoritomo first shogun in Japan

EUROPE	
c.6500	Farming begins in Greece and the Aegean
c.2000	Bronze Age in north Europe
c.2000–1200	Minoan and Mycenean civilization in Crete and Greece
753	Rome founded
c.750–c.550	Greeks and Phoenicians colonize Mediterranean and Black Sea
490–479	Battles of the Persian Wars
431–404	Peloponnesian War
c.380–300	Work of Plato, Euclid and Aristotle
c.327–300	Main Roman expansion
27	Octavian takes title of Augustus: end of Roman republic

AMERICA AND AUSTRALASIA BC	

AD

EUROPE	
c.43	Romans occupy Britain
284 305	Roman Empire reorganized and divided into East and West.
313	Freedom of Christian worship in Roman Empire
378	Valens defeated by Visigoths at Adrianople
410	Sack of Rome
496	Baptism of Clovis, king of the Franks
c.600	Slavs move into Balkans
711	Muslims invade Spain
768–814	Charlemagne builds Frankish empire
800s	Vikings invade and settle north-west Europe
1054	Break between Greek and Roman Churches
1066	Norman conquest
1096 1300	The Crusades

AMERICA AND AUSTRALASIA AD	
c.300–c.900	Mayan civilization in Central America
c.750	First Maoris arrive in New Zealand
c.1000	Greenland Vikings reach America
c.1325–1520	Aztec civilization in Mexico

H

H

AFRICA

1250	Mamluks seize power in Egypt
1300s	Mali Empire in west Africa
1400s and 1500s	European settlements on west coast
1500s	Songhai Empire replaced Mali Empire
1652	Dutch found Cape Colony
1869	Suez Canal opened
1880s	'Scramble for Africa'
1899–1902	Boer War
1914	All Africa except Liberia and Ethiopia colonized by European nations
1952–80	African states win independence
1981	President Anwar Sadat of Egypt is assassinated
1984–86	Severe famine in East Africa, millions face starvation
1985–86	Renewed unrest in South Africa results in international pressure for reform of apartheid
1986	US air raid on Libya strikes Tripoli and Benghazi

ASIA

1206–80	Mongols conquer empire in central Asia
1368–1644	Ming dynasty in China
1486–98	Voyages of Bartolomeu Dias and Vasco da Gama
c.1500–1870	African slave trade
1522–1680	Mughal expansion in India
c.1550–c.1650	Russians colonize Siberia
1630s	Japan isolates itself from rest of world
1644–1911	Manchu dynasty in China
1757	Battle of Plassey; British defeat French in India
1805	Beginning of East India Company's dominance in India
1839–42	Opium War; Britain takes Hong Kong
1857–9	Indian Mutiny
1867	Shoguns lose power in Japan
1900	Boxer Rebellion in China
1911	Republic established in China under Sun Yat-sen
1920–38	Career of Mustapha Kemal, Atatürk, in Turkey
1937	Japan invades China
1941	Japanese attack Pearl Harbor
1945	USA drops atomic bombs on Japan
1947	Indian independence
1948	State of Israel founded
1949	Communist victory in China.
1957–1973	Vietnam War
1979	Peace treaty signed between Israel and Egypt
1980	Iran-Iraq War
1982	Israel invades Lebanon
1984	Prime Minister Indira Gandhi of India is assassinated
1986	President Marcos' regime in the Philippines is overthrown. Nuclear reactor accident occurs at Chernobyl in the Ukraine

116

EUROPE

1337	Beginning of Hundred Years' War in France
1347–50	Black Death
c.1450	Gutenberg starts printing
1450–53	English driven out of France
1453	Constantinople falls to Ottoman Turks
1455–85	Wars of the Roses
1521	Martin Luther leads Protestant split from Roman Church
1618–48	Thirty Years' War
1642–48	English Civil War
1643–1715	Reign of Louis XIV
1750	Start of Industrial Revolution
1756–63	Seven Years' War
1789	French Revolution begins
1799	Napoleon seizes power in France
1815	Battle of Waterloo; Congress of Vienna
1821–29	Greek War of Liberation
1848	Year of revolutions throughout Europe
1854–6	Crimean War
1870–71	Franco-Prussian War
1885–95	Daimler and Benz work on automobile; Marconi's wireless
1914–18	World War I
1917	Bolshevik revolution in Russia begins
1933	Hitler becomes German Chancellor
1936–39	Spanish Civil War
1939–45	World War II
1941	Germany invades USSR
1945	Defeat of Germany. Cold War begins
1957	USSR launches first space satellite. Treaty of Rome: formation of European Economic Community
1980	Polish solidarity trade union confronts Communist government
1982	Argentina attempts takeover of Falkland Islands
1986	Prime Minister Olof Palme of Sweden is assassinated

AMERICA AND AUSTRALASIA

c.1400–1525	Inca civilization in Andes
1492	Columbus reaches America
1519	Cortes begins conquest of Aztec Empire
1532	Pizarro begins conquest of Inca Empire
1608	French colonists found Quebec
1620	*Mayflower* puritans (Pilgrim Fathers) settle in New England
1645	Tasman discovers New Zealand
1770	James Cook claims Australia for Britain
1776	American Declaration of Independence
1788	British colony founded at Botany Bay, Australia
1817–24	Careers of Simon Bolivar and José de San Martin
1840	Britain annexes New Zealand
1846–48	USA-Mexico War
1861–65	American Civil War
1898	Spanish-American War
1911	Mexican Revolution
1914	Panama Canal opened
1917	USA enters World War I
1929	Wall Street Crash begins Great Depression
1941	USA enters World War II
1945	United Nations set up
1959	Cuban Revolution
1963	President Kennedy assassinated
1969	Neil Armstrong lands on the Moon
1981	First Space Shuttle flight
1983	U.S. troops invade Grenada after Marxist takeover
1985	Earthquake in Mexico City claims 5000 lives
1986	Space shuttle *Challenger* explodes after take-off Jean Claude Duvalier's regime in Haiti is overthrown

H

HITLER, Adolf (1889–1945)

Hitler became 'Fuhrer' (leader) of Germany in 1933. He was an evil dictator whose Nazi party led Germany into World War II. German armies conquered most of Europe and millions of Jews were murdered on Hitler's orders. But Britain, the United States, the USSR and their allies defeated the Nazis. To avoid capture, Hitler killed himself.

HOCKEY

This is one of the most popular field games in the world. It can be played on any smooth, level surface in all seasons. It calls for speed, endurance and quickness of wit.

Hockey is played by two teams of 11 players a side. The object of the game is to hit a small, hard ball with a curved stick into the other team's goal.

HOMER

Two very famous poems called the *Iliad* and the *Odyssey* are said to have been the work of Homer. The poems were written in Greece about 800 BC. Both poems are about the Trojan War. The *Iliad* tells the story of how the Greeks captured the city of Troy. The *Odyssey* describes the homeward journey of the Greek hero Odysseus.

HORSE

The first horse was an animal no larger than a small dog. It is known as *Eohippus* or the 'dawn

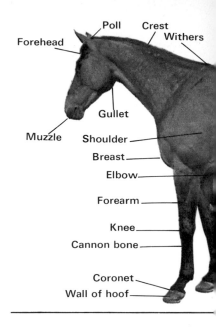

horse'. It had four toes on its front feet and three toes on its back feet. Gradually over millions of years, the horse lost all its toes except one.

No one knows when horses were first tamed. Their first use was to pull war chariots, and cavalry played an important part in wars until early in this century. Horses were the fastest form of transport until the 1800s when the steam locomotive and motor car replaced them. Also, their strength made horses invaluable on farms where they could pull wagons and ploughs.

Many different types of horses have been bred. Among the largest are the Shire and Clydesdale breeds. The Shetland pony is one of the smallest.

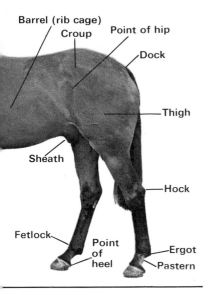

Barrel (rib cage)
Croup
Point of hip
Dock
Thigh
Sheath
Hock
Fetlock
Point of heel
Ergot
Pastern

HOVERCRAFT

A hovercraft is often called an air-cushion vehicle because it glides above the ground or water on a cushion of air. The cushion of air is created by a huge fan, which forces air beneath the craft. The air is held there by flaps or skirts around the sides.

▲ **The hovercraft** was invented in 1955 by Christopher Cockerell.

Backward-facing propellers on top of the craft propel it forwards and steer the craft. The propellers are powered by engines like those of an aircraft.

Some of the biggest hovercraft operate as car ferries across the English Channel. Each is 40 metres long and can carry 34 cars and 175 passengers.

HUMAN BEINGS

People exactly like us have lived for only a few thousand years. We belong to a group of mammals called the primates. Our scientific name is *Homo sapiens*, which means 'thinking man'.

Fossil remains of our primitive ancestors have been found in Africa and Asia. These early human-like creatures walked on two legs, and their skulls and teeth were quite like our own. But their brains were much smaller, about the same size as an ape's. After these 'ape-men', however, came creatures much more like modern human beings. They had bigger brains and they could use tools. Having a bigger brain made it possible for primitive people to develop until *Homo sapiens* appeared perhaps about 100,000 years ago.

The human brain gave human beings the power to hunt, kill, capture and tame other animals. Human beings developed skills far greater than those of any other creature. This made it possible for them to control the

Homo habilis

Homo erectus

Neanderthal man

Homo sapiens

environment in which they lived. They learned to make and use fire, to grow food and to make metal tools. They settled in villages and towns, and used language and writing to store and pass on the knowledge they had gained. In this way, civilization developed.

▲ **Four reconstructions** from fossils of the heads of early people.

HUMAN BODY

Our bodies are made of millions of tiny cells which are grouped together into separate tissues and organs. Skin protects us from heat, cold, injury and germs. Our bones give us our shape and allow us, with the help of our muscles, to move about.

Our bodies need oxygen and food. We get the oxygen from the air when we breathe. The blood carries the oxygen to every cell of the body. It also carries digested food, which is burnt by the oxygen to give us energy.

The body produces lots of waste. Some of this is excreted through the skin when we sweat, some (carbon dioxide) when we breathe out. Other waste is removed via the bowels and the bladder.

The only organs which are different in a man and a woman

▼ **This hummingbird** rolls its tongue into a tube to suck nectar from a flower.

are the reproductive organs. A woman has a vagina and ovaries which contain ova (eggs). A man has a penis and testes which contain sperm. The fertilization of a female egg cell by a male sperm cell produces one new cell which has all the makings of a complete new human body.

See also BLOOD; BRAIN; BREATHING; CELL; EAR; EYE; HEART; REPRODUCTION; SKIN.

HUMMINGBIRD
Hummingbirds are the smallest birds in the world. Most kinds live in the great forests of South America. Hummingbirds are marvellous fliers. They can hover in mid-air and even fly backwards. Their wings beat so fast they make a humming noise.

HYDROGEN
Hydrogen is an element. It is a colourless gas and has no smell and no taste. It is very light – more than 14 times as light as air. Hydrogen is easily set on fire.

Atoms of deuterium (heavy hydrogen) can be made to join together or *fuse* at a very high temperature to release huge quantities of energy. This is the principle of the hydrogen bomb.

HYENA
Hyenas are ungainly dog-like creatures. They live in Africa and Asia. They are useful scavengers. The strange howl of the laughing hyena sounds rather like weird human laughter.

ICE AGE
The Ice Ages were times of intense cold. Sheets of ice spread southwards from the North Pole, covering much of Europe, North America and Asia. The most recent Ice Age ended about 11,000 years ago. Glaciers (rivers of ice) carried soil and rocks along with them like huge bulldozers. They scraped the land clear of soil and smoothed hills and valleys.

During the recent Ice Age many plants and animals were killed by the cold. Human beings had to find ways of keeping warm. They took to the shelter of caves and made clothes from the skins of animals. In time the ice sheets melted and the weather grew warm again. But it is not certain that in the future there will never be another Ice Age.

See also GLACIER.

ICEBERG
Icebergs are islands of ice which drift in the cold polar seas. They are formed from masses of ice which break off the end of a glacier or ice sheet and float off into the sea. An iceberg can

121

weigh millions of tonnes. But only the tip of the iceberg shows above water. Five times as much is hidden beneath the surface.

See also GLACIER.

INCAS

Hundreds of years ago the Incas ruled an empire in the Andes mountains. Its heart lay in the South American country we now call Peru. All the people living in the mountain valleys had to work for the Incas. In return, the Incas made sure that everyone had a home and enough to eat.

▼ **A gold knife** used in Inca ceremonies.

▲ **A market** in the holy city of Varanasi (Benares), India.

The Incas became very rich. In 1532 Spanish explorers came seeking gold. They had horses and guns and they captured the Inca king, Atahualpa. They made themselves rulers of Peru.

INDIA

India is a large country, (about 3.28 million square kilometres). 750 million people live in India. The north is cut off from the rest of Asia by the Himalaya Mountains. Great rivers, such as the Brahmaputra and Ganges flow across the plains south of these mountains.

Parts of India are dry and hot. It is cooler in the mountains, but most people live in the fertile river valleys. India gets most of its rain during the monsoon season. Many Indians are poor farmers, who live in small villages. Others live in crowded cities like Calcutta. Industry is developing in India. There are steelworks, mines, textile and engineering factories.

Most Indians follow the Hindu religion. But there are also Buddhists, Sikhs, Muslims and Christians. Civilization began 4500 years ago in the area that includes India. From the late 1700s until 1947 most of India was ruled by Britain. Then it became independent.

See also GANDHI and page 65.

▶ **The growth cycle** of an insect.

▼ **The parts** of an insect.

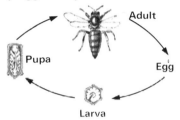

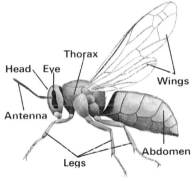

or *thorax*, carries three pairs of jointed legs and sometimes two pairs of wings as well. The end part is called the *abdomen*.

Most insects reproduce by laying eggs. Instead of bones, they have a hard case covering the outside of their bodies. As the insect grows, it has to shed this case and grow another.

Some young insects develop into adults without changing shape. They are called *nymphs*. But many kinds of insects go through two big changes in shape. At each stage, the insect looks different and has a different way of life. Butterflies lay eggs. They hatch into larvae called caterpillars. A caterpillar grows and turns into a pupa, or chrysalis. Finally, the adult butterfly emerges from the pupa. This process of change is known as *metamorphosis*.

Some insects are harmful. Insects such as the mosquito and the tsetse fly carry diseases. But many insects are useful. Bees and other insects pollinate flowers. The silkworm makes silk.

See also ANT; BEE; BEETLE; BUTTERFLIES AND MOTHS; FLY; GRASSHOPPER; MOSQUITO; PARASITE; WASP.

INSECT

Insects are found in every part of the world. There are hundreds of thousands of different kinds of insects, but they are all built on a similar plan. The body is divided into three sections. An insect's *head* has eyes, jaws and antennae, or feelers. The middle part,

INVENTION

Throughout history people have created new things. Most of these new products, or inventions, have given us an easier and better life. We can all benefit from machines and equipment, such as cars and aeroplanes, radio and television, papers and books. But some inventions, such as guns and bombs, are very destructive.

Many inventors invent to fulfil a need. James Hargreaves saw the need for a machine to spin cotton quicker, and he invented the spinning jenny.

Other inventors just seem to invent for the love of it. The American Thomas Edison was one of these. In his lifetime he registered, or patented, more than a thousand inventions.

Inventions are often the product of many people. The aeroplane was first flown by the Wright brothers, but they did not invent most of its parts. They drew upon the work of others who had gone before. The German engineers Daimler and Benz built the first successful cars by extending other people's ideas and adding some of their own.

See also EDISON; GALILEO; GUTENBERG; MARCONI; WATT.

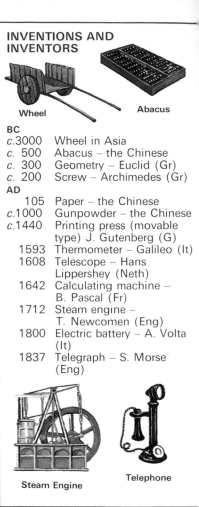

INVENTIONS AND INVENTORS

Wheel

Abacus

BC

c.3000	Wheel in Asia
c. 500	Abacus – the Chinese
c. 300	Geometry – Euclid (Gr)
c. 200	Screw – Archimedes (Gr)

AD

105	Paper – the Chinese
c.1000	Gunpowder – the Chinese
c.1440	Printing press (movable type) J. Gutenberg (G)
1593	Thermometer – Galileo (It)
1608	Telescope – Hans Lippershey (Neth)
1642	Calculating machine – B. Pascal (Fr)
1712	Steam engine – T. Newcomen (Eng)
1800	Electric battery – A. Volta (It)
1837	Telegraph – S. Morse (Eng)

Steam Engine

Telephone

IRELAND

Northern Ireland is part of the United Kingdom. Southern Ireland is a republic. In the republic most people are Roman Catholics. Most of the people in Northern Ireland are Protestants.

Ireland is mainly a farming country. It has fertile soil and a mild, moist climate. The centre of Ireland is flat, but there are mountains near the coast.

Ireland has had a troubled history. From the 1500s it was

Gunpowder

Printing Press

1836	Revolver – S. Colt (US)
1866	Dynamite – A. Nobel (S)
1876	Telephone – A. Bell (Sc)
1879	Electric light – T. Edison (US)
1887	Motor car engine – K. Benz, G. Daimler (G)
1895	Wireless – G. Marconi (It)
1899	Tape recorder – V. Poulsen (Den)
1925	Television – J. L. Baird (Sc)
1944	Digital computer – H. Aitken (US)
1960	Laser – T. Maiman (US)

Eng = England; G = Germany; It = Italy; Gr = Greece; Neth = Netherlands; Fr = France; US = America; Sc = Scotland; Den = Denmark; S = Sweden

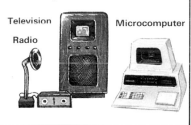

Television   Microcomputer

Radio

ruled by England. Many Irish people were poor and thousands emigrated to England and the United States. In 1921, 26 of the 32 Irish counties set up an independent country, which became the Republic of Ireland in 1949. Many people in the south want the six northern counties to become part of the republic. In Northern Ireland quarrels between Protestants and Catholics have led to fighting, bombings, murders and riots.

IRON AGE
This is the name given to a period when people began to use iron to make knives, axes and swords. Iron was first used about 2300 BC in Asia Minor. It reached Britain in about 500 BC. The Iron Age followed the Bronze Age.

Iron ores are found in many places in the world and can be smelted (made into iron) fairly simply on charcoal fires.

See also BRONZE AGE.

IRON AND STEEL
Steel is our most important metal. No other metal that is so strong is so cheap.

Steel is not a pure metal. It is an alloy made up mainly of iron, together with small amounts of carbon and one or two metals. Iron by itself is quite soft and weak, but adding the other ingredients makes it hard and strong.

Steel is like iron in other ways. It is magnetic, and it rusts easily. But by adding metals, such as chromium and nickel, we can make a steel that does not rust. It is called stainless steel.

Iron is found in the form of a mineral, or ore, in the ground. Crude iron is made in a blast

125

furnace by heating iron ore with coke and limestone. Steel is made by purifying the crude iron in other furnaces.

See also ALLOY.

▼ **Giant steel-making** machinery.

IRRIGATION

Irrigation waters the land to help crops to grow. In many places not enough rain falls each year, or it rains only at certain times of the year. Farmers have to get their water from rivers, wells or lakes.

The ancient civilizations of Egypt, India, China, Assyria and Babylon depended on irrigation. Today, engineers build dams to make artificial lakes. The water can then be released into pipes, earth channels or river systems as it is needed.

▶ **Milan Cathedral** in Italy.

ITALY

On the map Italy looks like a boot sticking out into the Mediterranean Sea. The islands of Sardinia and Sicily are also part of Italy. In the north the Alps form a mountain wall between Italy and the rest of Europe.

Southern Italy is warm and fairly dry. In the north it is cooler, with more rain. Both agriculture and industry are important. Most of the factories are in northern Italy. Italy is famous for its wine and for 'pasta' – foods such as spaghetti, macaroni and ravioli.

Most Italians are Roman Catholics. The centre of the Catholic Church is the Vatican, a tiny independent state in the middle of Rome. Italy has many old and beautiful buildings. A lot of them are in Rome, because 2000 years ago the Romans ruled Italy. Later separate city states grew up. The greatest were Genoa, Florence and Venice.

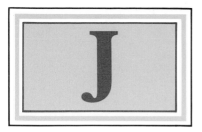

JAPAN

The islands which make up the country of Japan lie off the north-east coast of Asia. The largest islands are Honshu, Hokkaido, Kyushu and Shikoku. Earthquakes are common and there are volcanoes and hot springs. Japan has heavy rainfall and a cool climate.

Most Japanese live in cities. Rice, fish and vegetables are the main foods. There are many factories making all kinds of goods from cars and ships to radios and zip fasteners.

The Japanese came from mainland Asia perhaps 3000 years ago. Ancient Japan was ruled by warrior lords. Until the 1850s Japan had little contact with the world outside. But then its rulers decided to allow trade with European countries.

Japan became powerful, and its rulers became warlike. In World War II Japan joined Germany and Italy and Japanese forces conquered much of Asia. But in 1945 Japan surrendered. Today Japan's Emperor no longer has any power. There is an elected parliament and a government led by a prime minister.

See also page 64.

▼ The highest mountain in Japan, Mount Fuji, is an old volcano.

JELLYFISH

A jellyfish looks like a transparent umbrella floating in the sea. The body of this sea animal is mostly water. If it is stranded on the beach, a jellyfish dies.

Jellyfish swim by squirting out water from their 'umbrellas'. They catch other sea animals with stinging tentacles which hang beneath their bodies.

JENNER, Edward (1749 – 1823)

Jenner was an English physician. He discovered that people who had had cowpox, a mild disease, never caught smallpox, a painful and dangerous disease. He developed a vaccine from cowpox germs which protected people from smallpox.

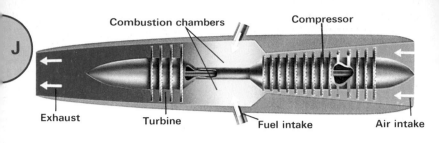

Combustion chambers   Compressor

Exhaust   Turbine   Fuel intake   Air intake

▲ **A gas turbine** jet engine. Air is drawn into the engine and compressed. Fuel is sprayed into the combustion chambers and burns in the air. The gases expand and drive the turbine. The gases leaving the engine thrust it forwards.

JESUS CHRIST

Jesus Christ was the founder of Christianity. Christians believe that he was the son of God. He taught people to trust in God and lead good peaceful lives and he promised eternal life in heaven. He performed miracles, healing the sick and making blind men see again. Jesus' followers said he was the Messiah. But others feared he was just a troublemaker. The Romans, who were the harsh rulers of the Jews, thought so too. Jesus was arrested and executed on the Cross. But his followers went on teaching others what he had taught them, even though the Romans at first tried to stop them. Many of these early Christians died for their belief in Jesus.

JET ENGINE

The jet engine was developed by both Britain and Germany. In 1930, Frank Whittle, a British engineer, patented the first gas-turbine for jet propulsion. Germany flew the first successful jet aircraft, the Heinkel 168, in 1939.

The aircraft gas turbine consists of a rotating shaft with a compressor at the front and a turbine wheel at the back. When the shaft turns, air is drawn into the engine and compressed. It enters combustion chambers where it mixes with liquid fuel such as paraffin. This mixture burns. The hot gases produced are allowed to escape from the back of the combustion chamber. As the fast jet of gas moves backwards out of the exhaust, it thrusts the engine forward.

The jet engine is smaller and lighter than the piston engine which it has largely replaced. It works efficiently at high speeds and produces great power.

JOAN OF ARC (1412–1431)

In 1429, France was at war with England. Joan was a French girl who believed God told her to save France. She persuaded France's King Charles VII to let her lead his army and won five battles. But she was captured by the English and burnt as a witch.

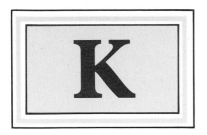

K

KANGAROO

Kangaroos live in Australia. They are the largest of the marsupials, the animals which carry their young in pouches.

Kangaroos eat grass and leaves. They travel about in groups called mobs, led by an old male known as a boomer. With their powerful hind legs and using their long tails to balance them, kangaroos can leap long distances.

▼ A kangaroo with its young, called a joey, in its pouch.

KENNEDY, John F. (1917–63)
John F. Kennedy was the 35th president of the United States. In 1961, he became the first Roman Catholic to be elected to this office. He tried to help the poor and underprivileged. He was assassinated in Dallas, Texas.

KING, Martin Luther (1929–68)
Martin Luther King was a black American clergyman and leader in the struggle for racial equality in the United States. Because he admired the teachings of Gandhi, he advised people not to use violence when they demonstrated against the segregation of black people. He won the Nobel Peace Prize in 1964. He was assassinated in 1968.

KINGS AND QUEENS

In the past most countries were ruled by 'monarchs': kings or queens. Usually the king's eldest son succeeded him, which meant that the same royal family might reign for hundreds of years.

English kings ruled with the help of their barons. In 1215 the barons forced King John to sign the Magna Carta, which said that the king should not misuse his powers. Later, English monarchs had to take the advice of Parliament. Britain is now a 'constitutional monarchy'. The Queen is the head of state, but her powers are limited by law. She *reigns* (holds office), but she does not *rule* (govern).

▲ **The kiwi** looks for food after dark.

KINGS AND QUEENS OF ENGLAND SINCE THE NORMAN CONQUEST (1066)

William I	1066–1087*
William II	1087–1100
Henry I	1100–1135
Stephen	1135–1154
Henry II	1154–1189
Richard I	1189–1199
John	1199–1216
Henry III	1216–1272
Edward I	1272–1307
Edward II	1307–1327
Edward III	1327–1377
Richard II	1377–1399
Henry IV	1399–1413
Henry V	1413–1422
Henry VI	1422–1461
Edward IV	1461–1483
Edward V	1483
Richard III	1483–1485
Henry VII	1485–1509
Henry VIII	1509–1547
Edward VI	1547–1553
Mary I	1553–1558
Elizabeth I	1558–1603

KINGS AND QUEENS OF GREAT BRITAIN FROM 1603

James I (VI of Scotland)	1603–1625
Charles I	1625–1649
Commonwealth	1649–1660
Charles II	1660–1685
James II	1685–1688
William III and (to 1694) Mary II	1689–1702
Anne	1702–1714
George I	1714–1727
George II	1727–1760
George III	1760–1820
George IV	1820–1830
William IV	1830–1837
Victoria	1837–1901
Edward VII	1901–1910
George V	1910–1936
Edward VIII	1936
George VI	1936–1952
Elizabeth II	1952–

* Dates refer to length of reign.

KIWI

The kiwi is the national bird of New Zealand. It cannot fly, but it waddles about the forest, searching for worms and insects to eat. The kiwi has hair-like feathers, no tail, strong claws and a long bill. It is the only bird that has nostrils at the tip of its bill.

▲ **A portrait** of Elizabeth 1, nicknamed Good Queen Bess.

KNIGHT

A knight in medieval times was a warrior who had vowed to be courageous yet gentle. This code of behaviour was called *chivalry*. A knight gave military service to a lord or an organization such as the church. In return, he was granted land.

130

The training to become a knight was long and severe. A boy of noble birth began as a page at the age of 7. At 14, he became a squire and began to learn the skills of a knight. He took vows of knighthood at about 21.

▲ **Young koalas** ride on their mother's back after leaving the pouch.

KOALA
Although it looks like a small bear, the koala is a marsupial. It lives in Australia. Koalas are good climbers. They live in eucalyptus trees, feeding on the leaves.

KORAN
The Koran is the holy book of Muslims. It is believed to have been dictated to Muhammed, the great prophet of Islam, by the archangel Gabriel. The Koran contains rules for both everyday and spiritual life. It was written down between AD 610 and 632.

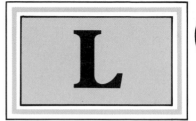

LAKE
Many lakes were formed during the Ice Ages by glaciers scooping out hollows in the land. When the ice melted, the hollows filled with water. Some lakes are artificial – created when dams are built across rivers.

Some lakes are so big that they are called seas. The Caspian Sea in Asia is the largest lake in the world. Its water is salty because the lake has no outlets. The water evaporates. The largest fresh water lake is Lake Superior in North America.

See also ICE AGE.

LANGUAGE
When we speak, we are using language. Language is a collection of 'sound signs' or words. We use it to communicate with one another. There are more than 2800 different languages in the world and many more *dialects* or local variations. Chinese is the language spoken by the largest number of people. English is spoken in more countries than any other language.

All languages change. People make up new words and often 'borrow' foreign words.

◀ **Laser beams** are very straight and narrow.

LATITUDE & LONGITUDE
Because we know that the world is round, we can show it on a globe and divide it into sections with accurately drawn lines.

The lines that run east and west and are parallel to the Equator are called *parallels* of latitude. Those that run north and south and pass through the poles are called *meridians* of longitude.

These lines are measured in degrees. By using these lines we can give the position of any place in the world. London is latitude 51° 30′ N, longitude 00° 05′ W.

LAW
All countries have rules which tell people how to behave and which must be obeyed. They make up the law of a country.

Law is made and works differently in different societies. In many countries groups of men and women are chosen by other people to make the laws. These people are called legislators and the law they make is *statute law*. Some law is made by judges. It is called *case law*. The law that comes from the customs of the people is called *common law*.

Lawyers are trained especially to understand the law. The job of the police and the courts is to arrest and punish people who break the law.

LASER
A laser is an instrument that produces a thin beam of very pure light. The beam from some lasers is so powerful that it can blast a hole through metal. Other lasers can be used in surgery to remove diseased body tissues, and to repair tissues in the eye.

An exciting new use of lasers is in communications. Laser beams can relay television signals and telephone messages. Sending telephone calls by laser may soon replace our present telephone system in which we send electric signals along copper wires.

132

LEAD

Lead is one of the heaviest metals. It is soft and easy to shape and does not rust. Lead is mixed with other metals to make useful alloys, such as pewter, which contains lead and tin. The metal used for printer's type contains lead. Solder used to join electrical wires and pipes also contains lead. And lead is also used in some car batteries.

See also ALLOY.

LEAF

All a plant's food is manufactured in its green leaves. Light, water and carbon dioxide are used to make a form of sugar. From the sugar the plant makes starch and other kinds of food that it needs.

The process that makes the food is called *photosynthesis*. It relies on the green colouring inside a leaf called *chlorophyll*. The carbon dioxide comes from the air. The water comes from the soil through tiny tubes called *veins*, and the carbon dioxide enters the leaf through little holes called *stomata*. The energy for photosynthesis comes from sunlight.

Leaves of plants growing in mild climates wither and fall off in the autumn. Lack of sunlight in winter makes them unnecessary. First the water supply to the leaves is cut off. This destroys the green colour and gives the leaves beautiful red, orange and brown tints.

DIFFERENT TYPES OF LEAVES

Hornbeam

Beech

Common oak

Horse chestnut

Sycamore

Common ash

LENIN, Vladimir (1870–1924)
Lenin is remembered as the man who made Russia a Communist country. When he was 17 Lenin decided to work against the Tsar (emperor) of Russia, because he thought the Tsar's rule was harsh and unjust. He became a Bolshevik (Communist) and in 1917 was the leader of the Communist Revolution.

LENS

A lens is a specially shaped piece of a transparent glass or plastic that refracts or bends rays of light. It makes an object look bigger or smaller. A lens which is thicker in the middle is called *convex*. It makes objects seen through it look bigger. A lens which is thicker at the edge is called *concave*. Objects seen through it look smaller.

LEONARDO DA VINCI
(1452–1519)

Leonardo was a great Italian artist, scientist and inventor. He was fascinated by the way in which the human body, machines, and the Universe worked. He designed war engines, a sort of helicopter, a parachute and diving gear. His *Last Supper* and *Mona Lisa* are among the best paintings in the world.

The cheetah of Africa is the fastest land animal. It hunts by stalking its prey and then chasing it at great speed. Not even the swift antelope can escape, for the cheetah can run at over 110 kilometres an hour, though only in short bursts.

Leopards and cheetahs both belong to the cat family.

▼ **The leopard** lives in wooded areas of Africa and Asia, the cheetah on the African plains.

Leopard

Cheetah

LEOPARD AND CHEETAH
The leopard lives in Africa and Asia. It is an expert tree climber and sometimes lies in wait for its prey in a tree. It can drag a half-eaten antelope into the branches out of reach of hyenas.

LICHEN

You often see a grey crust on rocks and tree trunks. It is made of tiny plants called lichens. A lichen is really two plants in one. One part is a fungus. The other part is a green plant called an alga. The fungus cannot make its own food. Instead it takes in water and minerals for the alga. The alga uses the water and sunlight to make food for itself and the fungus.

torch beam round a corner with a mirror. Light also bends when it passes from air into glass or water. This is called *refraction*. The bending of light by curved pieces of glass, or lenses, makes it possible to magnify objects, as in the microscope and telescope. When light is bent by a wedge of glass (a prism), it splits up into bands of colour. A laser is a powerful beam of very pure light.

See also COLOUR; LASER; SUN.

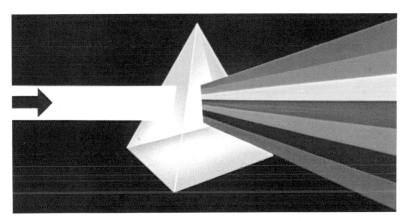

LIGHT

The Sun is a huge furnace that gives out vast amounts of energy as heat and light. Its light is one of the most important things to us on Earth. It enables us to see by day. We see things because objects reflect light into our eyes. Sunlight also gives green plants the energy to make their food. And all animals, including ourselves, rely on plant food to live.

Light travels in straight lines – you cannot shine a torch round a corner. But you can reflect the

▲ **White light** splits into the seven colours of the rainbow, the spectrum, when it is shone through a prism.

LIGHTNING

Lightning is a gigantic electric spark that zig-zags between the clouds in a thunderstorm. It also travels down to the ground, where it can cause great damage. It can split trees and set fire to buildings. Tall buildings have to be protected from lightning by a lightning conductor.

LINCOLN, Abraham
(1809–1865)

Lincoln began life poor, but became one of the most famous presidents of the United States. He hated slavery, and led the North to victory against the South in the American Civil War. He was assassinated by John Wilkes Booth, a supporter of the South, in 1865.

See also CIVIL WAR.

LINDBERGH, Charles
(1902–1974)

Lindbergh was an American pilot who performed a remarkable feat of daring and endurance. He flew non-stop in his single-engine plane, *The Spirit of St Louis*, from New York to Paris in May, 1927. The flight took 33½ hours and caught the imagination of the world.

LION

The lion is called 'the king of beasts'. With the tiger, it is the largest member of the cat family.

▼ **A lion and lioness** dozing in the African sun.

Lions live in groups called *prides*. Only the males have manes. The females, called lionesses, do most of the hunting.

Lions feed mainly on antelopes and zebras. They creep up on their prey and kill it after a short chase.

Lions once lived in Europe. Now wild lions are found only in parts of Africa and in a special reserve in India.

Frilled lizard
(Australia)

Marine Iguana
(Galapagos Islands)

LISTER, Joseph (1827–1912)
Lister was an English surgeon who did much to make operations safe. He used carbolic acid to clean instruments and to kill germs. He was also the first person to use catgut in surgery for stitching wounds.

LIZARD
Lizards are reptiles. Most lizards have four legs, but some are legless. The slow worm is a legless lizard. Unlike snakes, lizards have movable eyelids and visible ears.

Lizards generally live in warm climates. Most kinds lay eggs, but some produce live young. Lizards feed on insects, small mammals or plants. They prefer dry land, but the marine iguana is a good swimmer.

See also CHAMELEON; DINOSAUR; REPTILE.

LLAMA
The llama looks like a small woolly camel without a hump. It lives in the Andes mountains of South America.

Llamas are useful because they can carry loads along narrow mountain tracks. They also provide people with meat, wool, skins for making leather, and fat for candles.

LUTHER, Martin (1483–1546)
Luther was a monk who thought the Roman Catholic Church had moved too far away from the teachings of the Bible. He also objected to the custom of selling people pardons for their sins. Many Christians agreed with Luther. They started a great religious movement – the Reformation.

See also REFORMATION.

137

M

MACHINES, SIMPLE

Machines are devices that put energy to work. Most machines are complicated devices, but they are all based on six types of simple machine: the lever; the inclined plane; the wheel and axle; the pulley; the wedge; and the screw (see illustrations, right).

Starting from these simple machines, engineers have developed machines which can do a vast range of things. All machines, whether the simple lever or a giant crane, make it possible for people to do things more quickly and easily than they could by hand.

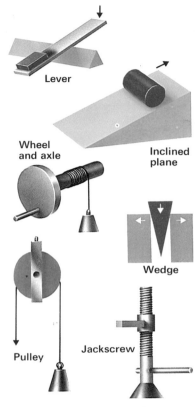

SIMPLE MACHINES

MAGELLAN, Ferdinand

(1480–1521)

Magellan was a Portuguese navigator in the service of Spain. He sought a sea route westwards to the Moluccas where spices were grown. He set out with four ships, found the route to the Pacific through what he named the Magellan Strait and went on to the Philippines. There he was killed by natives. One of his ships completed the first voyage round the world in 1522.

MAGIC

Before people understood what caused such things as storms or disease, many thought that nature was controlled by good and evil spirits. They believed that magic gave them power over these spirits. Some magic was good, or 'white'; but other magic was bad, or 'black'. The clever tricks of stage magicians and conjurors today really have nothing to do with magic.

MAGNET

Magnets can pick up or attract pieces of metal, particularly iron and steel. This power is called magnetism. The magnetism is most powerful at the ends of the magnet. If you hang a bar magnet from thread, it always points its ends towards the Earth's North and South magnetic poles. So we call the two ends its north and south poles. The magnet always points North-South because the Earth itself acts like a giant magnet. And one magnet affects another. The needle in a compass is a magnet.

MAMMAL

Mammals are the most advanced animals. They are vertebrates (animals with backbones) and they are warm-blooded. They can control the temperature of

▼ **This lamb** is a mammal.

▲ **This mammoth** was preserved in the frozen soil of Siberia.

their bodies by sweating or panting when it is hot and shivering when it is cold. Because of this, mammals can live in hot and cold climates. They have hairy or furry skins.

Almost all mammals, including human beings, give birth to live young, rather than eggs. The female feeds the young with milk from her body, and cares for them until they can look after themselves.

Mammals range in size from tiny shrews to huge whales. Most mammals are land animals, but dolphins and whales spend all their lives in the sea.

MAMMOTH

The mammoth was a hairy elephant. It lived during the Ice Age but is now extinct. Mammoths had long woolly hair and a thick layer of fat to keep out the cold. Prehistoric people hunted mammoths for food and drew pictures of them inside caves.

MAO ZEDONG (MAO TSE-TUNG) (1893–1976)

Modern China was founded by a farmer's son, Mao Zedong. He led the peasants in a revolution which changed China's government and way of life. He became a Communist, and for many years the Communists fought against the government. Mao was their leader, and in 1949 he led his armies to victory. China became a Communist state.

See also COMMUNISM.

MAP

A map is a drawing which shows all or part of the Earth's surface. It can show how cities, roads, railways, rivers, mountains and other features are arranged on the land.

A flat map cannot be really accurate because the Earth is round. Maps are drawn by various methods called *projections*.

▼ **These drawings** show how difficult it is to make an accurate map. When the surface of the round Earth is stretched out, some parts must be squashed out of shape or distorted.

Maps are drawn to scale. For example, a distance of one centimetre on the map may represent a kilometre on the ground.

Political maps show countries, and often cities, roads and railways. Physical maps show mountains, rivers and other land features.

MARCONI, Guglielmo (1874–1937)

Marconi worked with and made important discoveries about radio waves. He patented wireless telegraphy and, in 1901, he sent the first wireless message across the Atlantic.

MARCO POLO (c.1254–1324)

The book, *The Travels of Marco Polo*, recorded the adventures of this Venetian merchant. With his

father and his uncle he journeyed to China in 1275. The Emperor, Kublai Khan, favoured Marco and made him first a court attendant and later an official. He served the Emperor for 17 years. They returned home in 1295 bringing with them great wealth.

MARSUPIAL
Marsupials are primitive mammals. Most marsupials live in Australia and New Guinea. The opossum lives in the Americas.

A marsupial is born tiny. It crawls into its mother's pouch, where it sucks milk until it is big enough to leave.

MARX, Karl (1818–83)
Marx was the founder of the modern Communist movement. His writings greatly changed the way many people thought about society. He helped write *The Communist Manifesto* in 1848 arguing that all old forms of government had to be overthrown. In *Das Kapital* he wrote that working people should rule and run the factories.

MATHEMATICS
Mathematics is a science that deals with numbers and shapes. Arithmetic is one branch of mathematics. The other main branches are algebra, geometry, trigonometry and calculus. Arithmetic deals with figures. Algebra deals with figures and symbols. Geometry deals with shapes. Trigonometry deals with measurement of triangles and problems based on this. Calculus deals with changing quantities.

M

▲ **The swamp wallaby** is a marsupial.

MEASUREMENT
How long is your desk? How heavy are you? How much water is in the bottle? We find the answers to these questions by measurement. We measure by using devices or instruments marked with a scale of numbers. To measure length we use a rule. For weight, we use a pair of scales. For volume, we use a measuring jug.

Although the numbers on the various scales may be the same, they mean different things. On the rule, 20 may mean 20 centimetres; on the pair of scales, 20 kilogrammes; and on the jug, 20 millilitres. The centimetre, kilogramme and litre are different units of measurement. They are units of length, weight, and volume in the metric system of measurement. The metric system is one in which the units go up in steps or multiples of 10.

MEDICINE

Since very early times people have searched for medicines to heal wounds and cure diseases. The first drugs came from berries and herbs which had healing powers.

The ancient Greeks and Romans knew what the inside of the human body looked like. But they did not know how the different parts worked, or what made them go wrong.

Medicine made little progress until the 1600s, when doctors began studying anatomy (the parts of the body). By cutting up dead bodies, they began to find out how the body works. But since no one knew about germs, doctors did not bother very much about cleanliness. Many patients died because hospitals were dirty places.

Over the next 200 years progress in medicine was slow. But in the 1700s *vaccination* was discovered as a way of preventing disease, and later *antiseptics* were developed to kill harmful germs. *Anaesthetics* came to be used to deaden pain during operations. In the 1900s the discovery of X-rays meant that doctors could examine the insides of their patients to find out what was wrong without cutting them open. Powerful new drugs called *antibiotics* were also discovered.

See also DISEASE; DRUGS; X-RAYS.

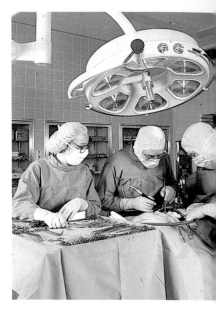

▲ **A patient** undergoing surgery in a sterilized operating theatre.

ADVANCES IN MEDICINE

1593	Thermometer – Galileo
1590	Microscope – Zacharias Janssen
1628	Blood circulation – William Harvey
1796	Vaccination – Edward Jenner
1846	Anaesthetic – William Morton
1865	Antiseptic surgery – Joseph Lister
1877	Germs cause disease – Louis Pasteur
1895	Psychoanalysis – Sigmund Freud
1895	X-rays – William Roentgen
1898	Radium – Pierre and Marie Curie
1928	Penicillin – Alexander Fleming

MENDEL, Gregor (1822–1884)
Mendel was an Austrian monk who studied the way in which physical characteristics are passed on from parent to child. He observed that the colour and shape of peas were passed on from generation to generation according to certain laws.

His discoveries went un-noticed until improved microscopes made it possible to see chromosomes, the minute thread-like bodies which carry these hereditary characteristics.

See also GENETICS.

METALS

There are over 60 different metals. They make up the most important group of elements. They are very different from the other elements. Metals pass on, or conduct, electricity and heat well. Most non-metals do not. Many metals have a silvery, shiny surface. They are tough and strong, but can be bent and hammered without breaking.

Most metals are found in the form of mineral ores. They must be separated out before they can be used. There are several different ways of taking, or extracting, a metal from its ore. Iron is extracted by smelting, aluminium by means of electricity.

Metal may be shaped by casting, hammering, rolling, forcing through holes and cutting.

See also ALUMINIUM; COPPER; GOLD; IRON AND STEEL; MINING.

▲ **Electricity** is used to extract aluminium from bauxite.

METEOR

On some nights you may see bright streaks in the sky. Though they look like falling stars, these glowing trails are actually made by meteors, lumps of rock or metal. As they shoot through the upper part of the Earth's atmosphere they burn up in a flash of light.

▼ **An unusually** bright meteor display.

143

MEXICO

Mexico is a republic and lies just south of the United States. Most of it consists of a broad, central plateau that is flanked on both sides by mountain ranges. On the west is the Pacific Ocean and on the east, the Gulf of Mexico and the Caribbean Sea. There are three main kinds of climate – cool, temperate and hot – and a huge variety of plant life.

Over a third of Mexico's 78,524,000 people work on the land, growing mostly maize, beans, coffee, wheat, cotton, sugar and vegetables.

Mexico is rich in minerals. Its silver and gold originally attrac-ted the Spanish. There is also oil. Mexico's factories produce a wide variety of goods.

MICHELANGELO
(1475–1564)

Michelangelo was a sculptor, architect, painter and poet who lived in Italy at the time of the Renaissance. Among his most famous statues are the *Pieta* and *David*. He painted a scene on the ceiling of the Sistine Chapel in the Vatican depicting the creation of the world.

See also RENAISSANCE.

▼ **A sculpture** by Michelangelo.

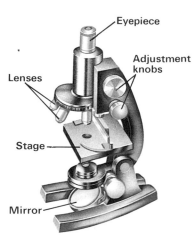

▲ **An optical microscope.** It has a base, a tube containing the lenses, and a body, or upright, to hold the tube. Objects to be studied are put on glass slides.

- Eyepiece
- Adjustment knobs
- Lenses
- Stage
- Mirror

MICROSCOPE

A microscope makes small objects look bigger, so that we can see things that are invisible to the naked eye.

Ordinary microscopes magnify by bending light rays with glass lenses. The bent rays make an image which is bigger than the original object. Electron microscopes are much more powerful than ordinary microscopes, and can magnify things hundreds of thousands of times. They magnify by bending beams of electrons, rather than light rays.

See also LENS; LIGHT.

MIDDLE AGES

The Roman Empire fell in AD 476 and it took 1000 years for strong nations to grow out of the confusion that followed. In between lay the Middle Ages. In the early Middle Ages, Europe was overrun by barbarians. They sacked and burned towns, and soon the art and learning of Rome was forgotten, except by monks.

To defend themselves, people banded together under the protection of strong leaders, or kings. The peasants became the vassals of rich nobles and knights. They traded crops and services for protection. The nobles became vassals of the king. In return for the king's protection they promised to supply soldiers in war. This is known as the *feudal system*.

Life in the Middle Ages was often harsh and cruel. Anyone who broke the law was severely punished. And anyone who questioned the Church's teachings was punished harshly too.

But slowly knowledge grew. Beautiful cathedrals were built. Universities and schools were founded. Gradually government became more settled, and trade flourished. With the voyages of discovery in the 1400s and the Renaissance, the Middle Ages came to an end.

▲ **This illuminated picture** is from the *Book of Hours* made in the 15th century. Each month is illustrated with a scene showing life in the Middle Ages.

MIDDLE EAST

The desert lands of south-west Asia and north-east Africa are often called the Middle East. This area stretches from Egypt to

Iran. Most of the people are Muslim Arabs. Many are poor, but oilfields have made some Middle East countries rich.

In 1948 the Jews founded the state of Israel in what had been British-ruled Palestine. The Arabs would not accept this. There have been five wars between Israel and the Arab countries, in 1948, 1956, 1967 1973 and 1982.

See also COUNTRIES OF THE WORLD.

MIGRATION

Many swallows spend the summer in Europe. But in the autumn they fly south to the warmth of Africa. This journey is called migration.

Many animals migrate to find food or to breed. Caribou move south to escape the Arctic winter. African antelope migrate during the dry season to find water and fresh grass.

Some birds fly very long distances. The Arctic tern flies from the Arctic winter to the Antarctic summer, and back again.

Frogs, toads and newts spend most of their time on land. But they return to ponds and streams to lay their eggs.

MINERAL

A mineral is any substance that can be mined. There are nearly 3000 kinds of minerals. Some, such as gold and silver, are pure

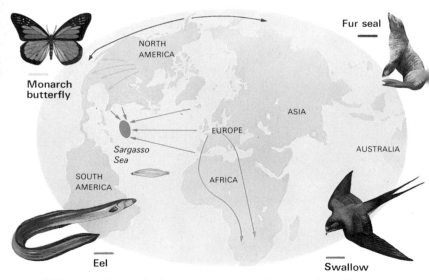

Fur seal

Monarch butterfly

NORTH AMERICA

ASIA

EUROPE

Sargasso Sea

AUSTRALIA

SOUTH AMERICA

AFRICA

Eel

Swallow

▲ **This map** shows the journeys made by some animals in autumn. The eel is the only one not to return in spring. It breeds and dies in the Sargasso Sea. But the young elvers will eventually return to the rivers their parents once lived in.

146

elements. But most, such as salt and coal, are combinations of the 92 naturally occurring elements. Pure minerals are made up of atoms arranged in regular patterns known as crystals. This is what makes jewels like diamonds and emeralds sparkle.

See also DIAMONDS; GEMS; MINING.

MINING

Mining means taking minerals from the ground. It is one of our most important industries and supplies many other industries with their raw materials.

Sometimes mineral deposits can be dug out from the surface. Other deposits lie just below the surface. The soil is first stripped off, then explosives break up the deposits. Power shovels load the mineral into trucks.

Often the mineral deposits are buried deep in the ground. Miners have to travel by lift down shafts and in trains along tunnels to reach them.

MOLE

A mole is a small mammal which lives underground almost all its life. Its eyes are very weak and it uses its ears, nose and delicate touch organs to find its way about. It eats worms and grubs.

MOLLUSC

Molluscs are animals with soft bodies. To protect themselves, many molluscs have shells.

Some molluscs, like the mussel, stay inside their shells and hardly ever move. Others, such as the cockle, use their single foot to move around. Snails and slugs crawl very slowly.

The largest and most active molluscs are the octopus, which has no shell, and the squid, which has its shell inside its body.

▲ **Moles** spend most of their lives underground and are blind.

MONASTERY

A monastery is the home of a religious community. The monks who live in the monastery take religious vows promising not to marry, not to have possessions or money, and do whatever work they are asked to do. They spend the day working, studying or in prayer. The long tunic many monks wear is known as a *habit*.

147

The first Christian monasteries were started about 200 years after the death of Christ. By the Middle Ages there were several important 'orders' of monks and friars (friar means brother).

Some monks work outside the monastery as missionaries and teachers. Others remain in the monastery and lead strict lives.

MONEY

Originally, people did not use money. They bartered or traded. When people settled in towns, trade became more complicated. The barter system was too clumsy. So *token goods*, such as

▼ **A selection** of coins from different countries.

cattle or shells, were used. This was the beginning of the money system. Later small pieces of metal, or coins, came into use.

Merchants in the Middle Ages began to exchange pieces of paper, promising payment for goods bought. They set up banks, in which to keep their gold safe. The banks began to issue paper money, or bank notes, and people gradually accepted that these had the same value as gold.

Today, the government controls how much money is made by minting coins and printing notes. The money we use is token money: that is, modern coins are made of cheap metals and have little value in themselves. The real value of money is the amount of goods it will buy.

See also COIN.

MONKEY

Monkeys belong to the group of animals called primates. Old World monkeys live in Africa and Asia. New World monkeys live in Central and South America. New World monkeys have *prehensile* tails, which can grasp a branch like an extra hand. Old World monkeys cannot do this.

Monkeys are lively, intelligent animals. They use their hands and feet to hold things. Most monkeys live in groups. They eat fruit and other parts of plants, insects, small mammals and birds' eggs.

MONKEYS

Black howler monkey

Long-nosed proboscis monkey

Squirrel monkey

Golden Spider monkey

MOON

The Moon is a ball of rock, about a quarter the diameter (width) of the Earth. It has no atmosphere. Because there is no air there is no weather on the Moon, and no sound. There is no water and no life at all. It is very hot in the sunlight, but icy cold in the shade.

The Moon's surface is not smooth. There are great, flat plains and jagged peaks and mountain ranges. Everywhere on the Moon there are pits, or craters. The whole surface is covered with loose rocks and a thick layer of fine dust.

The Moon travels around the Earth once a month. The shape of the Moon appears to change during the month. What changes is the area we can see which is lit by the Sun. This area changes because of the Moon's movement around the Earth.

See also ECLIPSE.

▼ **The Moon** shows 'phases' as it moves round the Earth. It takes $29\frac{1}{2}$ days to complete these phases, as more or less of its surface is lit by the Sun. First it waxes (from crescent, or new, moon to full moon) and then wanes (from full back to crescent).

MOSQUE

Mosques are the buildings in which the services of the religion Islam take place. Most mosques have a dome, a minaret, from which the faithful are called to prayer five times a day, and a prayer niche showing the direction of Mecca.

MOSQUITO

The mosquito is a fly with a small body and long legs. Some mosquitoes spread diseases such as malaria. The male is harmless. But the female mosquito feeds on the blood of animals, including human beings. The insect pours a juice into the wound to stop the blood clotting, or hardening, and this can pass on a disease.

Mosquitoes lay their eggs in water. In warm countries, where mosquitoes are most dangerous, the eggs and larvae are destroyed.

▼ **Muslims** worship God in a mosque. This one is in Iraq.

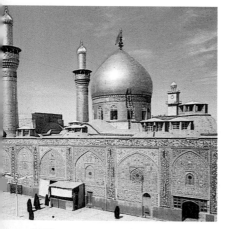

MOSS

Mosses are simple plants. They do not have flowers, but reproduce by sending out tiny offshoots. Spores, or cells, grow on these shoots. When the spores are ripe, they are blown away by the wind. New moss plants develop from them.

MOTOR CAR

Two German engineers, Karl Benz and Gottlieb Daimler, built the first cars in 1885 and 1886. These had a petrol engine, like most modern cars. Later, some cars were built with steam engines; others were driven by electricity from batteries. But in the end the petrol engine proved to be the most successful.

At first, cars were hand-made and expensive. It was not until 1908 that they began to be made cheaply. In that year Henry Ford started to mass produce his Model T, called the 'Tin Lizzie'. It marked the beginning of the modern car industry, which now produces over 25 million cars a year throughout the world.

A modern car is a collection of 10,000 or more separate parts. These parts make up several basic units: the body, the engine and the transmission are the main units. The transmission carries power from the engine to the driving wheels. The other units are the steering, the braking and the suspension.

See also FORD, Henry.

1770 Cugnot

1899 Renault

1886 Daimler

1910 Model T Ford

1961 E Type Jaguar

1981 Ford Fiesta

1935   Hispano Suiza

MOTORCYCLE

A motorcycle is a vehicle which has two and sometimes three wheels. The first motorcycles were built at the end of the 1800s when men such as Edward Butler, an Englishman, and Gottlieb Daimler, a German, began making powered bicycles and tricycles. The first motorcycle races in 1907 encouraged improvements in design which soon brought the motorcycle to something like its present form with electric ignition, variable gears and the engine mounted low down between the two wheels.

1894 Hildebrand and Wolfmuller

1980s Honda 500

▶ **On a mountain,** different plants grow in zones at various heights. On the lower slopes are deciduous trees. Higher up there are conifers. Above the tree line are shrubs, alpine flowers, and then lichens and mosses. Snow covers the highest peaks.

Snow-line

Tree-line

HIGHEST MOUNTAINS		South America	
		Aconcagua	6960
Asia	**Metres**	**North America**	
Everest	8848	McKinley	6194
Godwin Austen	8611	**Africa**	
Kanchenjunga	8597	Kilimanjaro	5895
Makalu	8470	**Europe**	
Dhaulagiri	8172	Elbruz	5633
Nanga Parbat	8126	Mont Blanc	4810
Annapurna	8075	**Antarctica**	
Gasherbrum	8068	Vinson Massif	5139
Gosainthan	8013	**Oceania**	
Nanda Devi	7817	Wilhelm	4694

MOUNTAIN

Mountains are masses of rock which rise at least 600 metres above the surrounding land.

Mountains are usually grouped together in ranges, chains or massifs. Some mountains are the cones of volcanoes. But most are formed by folding and sideways movements of the crust, or outer skin, of the Earth. These movements push up the rocks to build mountains. Mountain building takes millions of years. It is still going on today in parts of the Earth. The rocks are worn away by rain, wind, ice and snow.

The height of a mountain is always measured in height above sea level. The world's highest mountains are in the Himalayas in Asia. Mount Everest (8848 metres) is the highest.

MOZART, Wolfgang Amadeus (1756–91)

The Austrian composer Mozart was a musical genius. He began writing music at the age of five. Two years later his father took him to play at concerts in the great cities of Europe. Mozart wrote church music, opera and nearly 50 symphonies. He worked hard but earned little money and died very poor at the age of 35.

MUHAMMAD (AD 570–632)

The Arab prophet Muhammad founded the religion of Islam. He taught people to stop worshipping idols and follow the 'true God', called Allah. In 622 Muhammad's enemies drove him out of his birthplace, Mecca. He fled to the city of Medina, and converted many people to the new religion. By the time Muhammad died, Islam had spread throughout Arabia.

MUSHROOM & TOADSTOOL

These plants belong to the fungus group. Fungi are not green. They contain no chlorophyll, so they cannot use sunlight to make their food like other plants. Instead they feed on dead and decaying plant and animal matter. Some are parasites. Fungi have no flowers or seeds and reproduce by means of cells.

See also PHOTOSYNTHESIS.

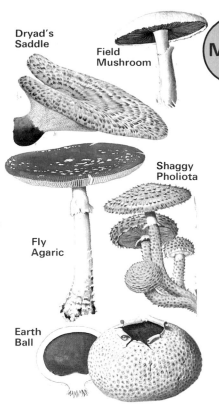

Dryad's Saddle

Field Mushroom

M

Shaggy Pholiota

Fly Agaric

Earth Ball

MUSIC

Music is a set of sounds arranged in a way that is pleasant to hear. It has rhythm (the beat), harmony (the total sound when several notes are played together) and usually melody (the tune). Music is made up of *notes* that may be long or short, loud or soft, high or low.

At first music had a simple melody and rhythm. But it gradually grew more complicated. Two or three tunes were played together. This rich sound was called *counterpoint*.

People who make up music and write it down are called *composers*. Two great composers of counterpoint were Bach and Handel. Much great music has been written for orchestras by composers such as Haydn, Mozart, Beethoven and Brahms. They wrote *symphonies* (long pieces of music for orchestras) and *chamber music* (for smaller groups of instruments). They also wrote music for choirs. Some composers have written operas – musical plays in which all the words are sung.

153

FAMOUS COMPOSERS

Antonio Vivaldi, Italian
(1678?–1741)
Johann Sebastian Bach,
German (1685–1750)
Wolfgang Amadeus Mozart,
Austrian (1756–1791)
Ludwig van Beethoven,
German (1770–1827)
Franz Schubert, Austrian
(1797–1828)
Hector Berlioz, French
(1803–1869)
Fréderic Chopin, Polish
(1810–1849)
Robert Schumann, German
(1810–1856)
Franz Liszt, Hungarian
(1811–1886)
Giuseppe Verdi, Italian
(1813–1901)
Richard Wagner, German
(1813–1883)
Johannes Brahms, German
(1833–1897)
Peter Ilich Tchaikovsky,
Russian (1840–1893)
Anton Dvorak, Czech
(1841–1904)
Edvard Grieg, Norwegian
(1843–1907)
Edward Elgar, British
(1857–1934)
Giacomo Puccini, Italian
(1858–1924)
Gustav Mahler, Austrian
(1860–1911)
Claude Debussy, French
(1862–1918)
Jean Sibelius, Finnish
(1865–1957)
Sergei Rachmaninov, Russian
(1873–1943)
Igor Stravinsky, Russian
(1882–1971)
Dmitri Shostakovich, Russian
(1906–1975)
Benjamin Britten, British
(1913–1976)

People often call this kind of music 'classical' music. There are many other kinds of music, including folk songs, jazz and pop music. Modern music is very different from the music of the 1800s. It has difficult rhythms and sounds, and sometimes requires electronic instruments as well as wind, stringed and percussion instruments.

See also BACH; BEETHOVEN; MOZART; OPERA.

MUSICAL INSTRUMENT
Musical instruments have been made for thousands of years. There are three main groups of instruments. *Wind instruments* are played by blowing down a hollow wooden or metal tube with holes cut in it. By covering some holes with the fingers, different notes are produced. Wind instruments include flutes, clarinets, trumpets and horns.

The *stringed instruments* have strings stretched across a hollow box. The strings are bowed, as in a violin, or plucked, as in a guitar, to make different notes. Short strings make high notes and long strings make low notes. Stringed instruments include violins, guitars, banjos and lutes.

Instruments such as drums, cymbals and bells, which are hit with hammers or sticks, are called *percussion instruments*.

See also ORCHESTRA.

MUSICAL INSTRUMENTS

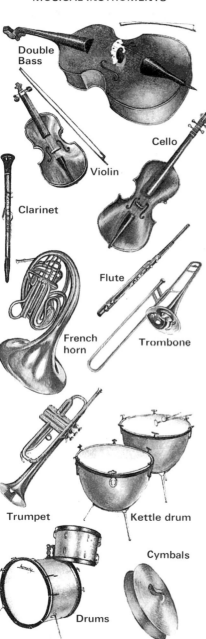

Double Bass

Cello

Violin

Clarinet

Flute

French horn

Trombone

Trumpet

Kettle drum

Cymbals

Drums

NAPOLEON BONAPARTE
(1769–1821)

After the French Revolution in 1789, Napoleon conquered much of Europe. In 1804 he made himself Emperor of France. But in 1812 his army had to retreat from Russia, and in 1815 the British and Prussians beat the French at the battle of Waterloo. He was exiled, and died on the island of St Helena.

NASSER, Gamal Abdel
(1918–70)

Nasser was an Egyptian revolutionary and army officer. He helped to depose King Farouk in 1952 and became president in 1956. He tried to modernize Egypt. In 1956 he nationalized, or took over, the Suez Canal.

NELSON, Horatio (1758–1805)
Nelson was a great British admiral whose statue stands above Trafalgar Square, London.

He fought and defeated the French fleet led by Napoleon near Alexandria in 1798 (the Battle of the Nile). His most famous battle was at Trafalgar in 1805 when he was shot and killed during this battle.

155

N

▲ **The nest** of the harvest mouse.

NEST
Many animals build nests for their young. Usually they are well hidden and out of reach of enemies. Some are simple, just scrapes in the ground or untidy piles of twigs. But many are elaborately built of mud, grass, moss, feathers and wax. Birds, fish, insects, reptiles and mammals build nests.

NETHERLANDS
The Netherlands is a small country in Europe. It is largely flat, but in the south and east there are low hills and moorlands.

The Netherlands is well known for its dikes and canals. Two-fifths of the country has been reclaimed from lakes,

▶ **The low-lying** Netherlands countryside is drained by dikes and canals.

marshes or the sea. The canals drain the land to make new land for farming. Much of the Netherlands is below sea level. Dikes keep the water out.

Dairy farming, horticulture and food-processing are very important, but industry has grown rapidly in recent years.

The Netherlands is a kingdom. See also page 64.

NEWTON, Isaac (1642–1727)
Newton was one of the greatest scientists and mathematicians the world has known. He was the first person to explain the force of gravity, which holds the Universe together. Newton carried out many experiments with light and split up light into a spectrum, or band of colour. He built the first reflecting telescope and he invented calculus.

Newton was born in England and studied mathematics and science at Cambridge University.

See also COLOUR; GRAVITY; LIGHT; TELESCOPE.

NEW ZEALAND

Two long and narrow islands, the North Island and South Island, and a few smaller islands make up the country of New Zealand. It lies in the south Pacific Ocean.

New Zealand has high mountains, volcanoes, hot springs, fast-flowing rivers and glaciers. Most of the towns and cities are on the coast. The climate is mild.

The grasslands are ideal for sheep and cattle farming. New Zealand is famous for its butter, cheese and meat, and for fruit.

The native Maoris settled in New Zealand about 700 years ago. Although the Dutch explorer Abel Tasman discovered and named New Zealand in 1642 the country was mainly settled by people from Britain.

See also page 65.

NIGERIA

Nigeria is a large country in West Africa. It has a tropical climate and the largest population in

Africa. Nigeria is a hot country. Much of the land is dry, grassy savanna but there are also mangrove swamps and forests along the coast.

Nigeria produces oil, hardwoods, palm oil, groundnuts, cocoa and various fruits and vegetables. A great variety of animals live in the country including gorillas, chimpanzees, lions and elephants.

Most Nigerians are Negroes who belong to different tribes. Many speak different languages. Nigeria is a member of the Commonwealth.

See also page 64.

NOBEL PRIZE

Every year six Nobel prizes may be awarded, for outstanding work in chemistry, physics, medicine, literature, economics and the cause of peace. Two or three people may share a prize, and the prizewinners may come from any part of the world. To win a Nobel prize is a very great honour. The money for the prizes was given by Alfred Nobel, a Swedish chemist, who invented the explosive dynamite.

NOMADS

Nomads are groups of people who wander from place to place with their animals and possessions. They do not build permanent houses. Some nomads keep flocks and herds and move to find fresh grazing land for their animals.

ALASKA

CANADA

Hudson Bay

Canadian Shield

Rockies

Prairies

Great Lakes

Grand Canyon

The Great Plains

NORTH AMERICA

Appalachians

Atlantic Ocean

MEXICO

Pacific Ocean

WEST INDIES

Caribbean Sea

CENTRAL AMERICA

Panama Canal

NORTH AMERICA

This is the third largest of the Earth's continents. It stretches from the cold wastes of Alaska in the north to the hot deserts of Mexico and the tropical forests of Central America in the south. Canada and the United States of America cover most of North America. North America covers about a sixth of the Earth's land surface.

Down the western side of North America run the rugged Rocky Mountains. In the centre of the continent are wide grasslands called prairies. The Canadian Shield, a wild region of lakes and forests in northern Canada, has valuable minerals, such as coal and oil. In the south of the continent are coastal plains, swampy in places. The longest river in North America is the Mississippi, which joins another long river, the Missouri. The Great Lakes are the largest fresh water lakes in the world.

Crops grown in North America include wheat, fruit, vegetables and cotton. Forestry and furs are important in the north, and fishing is a major activity. Canada and the United States are great industrial countries, with plentiful raw materials.

North America is a continent of great contrasts. It has some of the world's largest cities, such as Mexico City and New York. But there are huge areas with hardly any people at all. The United States is one of the richest countries in the world. But in Central America the countries are small and poor.

The first people in North America came from Asia. They were the ancestors of the American Indians and Eskimos. Much later Europeans came bringing with them Negro slaves from Africa. See also page 65.

NUCLEAR ENERGY

Under certain conditions atoms of uranium can be made to split. When they do so, large amounts of energy are released as heat and light. The splitting of the atom, or rather of its nucleus, is called nuclear fission.

Scientists can now control the fission of uranium and use the energy it releases to produce nuclear power. In furnaces, called reactors, great heat is produced when the nucleus of the atom splits. This heat is used to drive turbines and generate electricity. Nuclear power is also used to drive some ships.

In atomic bombs, the nuclear reaction is uncontrolled and all the energy is released, causing devastation over a huge area.

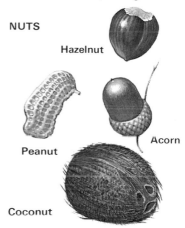

NUTS

Hazelnut

Acorn

Peanut

Coconut

NUT

Some trees bear fruits called nuts. Inside the tough shell of the nut is a seed. Many animals crack or gnaw at nuts to get at the seed inside. Ripe nuts fall to earth in autumn. The seed sends a new shoot pushing through the shell; and a new tree begins its life.

OASIS

An oasis is a fertile area in a desert. Sometimes water comes to the surface naturally. Sometimes wells are sunk to tap it. Some oases cover many square kilometres and may support a city. Others have only a few huts.

▼ **An oasis** on the desert coast of Peru, South America.

▲ **At its outer edge** the continental shelf plunges down to the ocean floor or abyss, a plain crossed by rivers and trenches

OCEANS

About 70 per cent of the Earth's surface is covered by water. The large areas of salty water which separate the continents are called oceans.

There are five oceans. The biggest and deepest is the Pacific Ocean, which separates America and Asia. Next come the Atlantic Ocean and the Indian Ocean. The Antarctic and Arctic Oceans surround the Poles.

Around most coasts a shelf of land runs out under the sea. This is the *continental shelf*. It lies up to 180 metres deep, and may stretch for hundreds of kilometres. Beyond the continental shelf, the ocean floor drops away steeply. It flattens out again at a depth of about 3650 metres. The bottom of the ocean is called the abyss. It is a flat plain, crossed by ridges, high mountains and deep trenches.

Life abounds in the oceans. Today, sea creatures range in size from enormous whales to tiny drifting animals, too small to be seen without a microscope. There are many plants, including huge seaweeds.

The oceans are never still. The rise and fall of the tides, which takes place roughly every twelve hours, is caused by the gravitational pull of the Earth and the Moon. The surface of the water is moved by waves, caused by the wind.

See also TIDE; WIND.

OIL
Oil is a greasy substance that does not mix with water. There are three kinds of oil: mineral, fatty and 'essential'.

Mineral oil is distilled from petroleum. It comes from the Earth's crust and is used for fuels and lubricants.

Fatty oils come from both animals and vegetables. Linseed oil, lard, butter and margarine are fatty oils.

Essential oils give scents and flavours to flowers and fruits. Lemon oil from lemon rind and cinnamon from bark are kinds of essential oils.

OLYMPIC GAMES
Between 776 BC and AD 393, the ancient Greeks held athletic contests at Olympia every four years. The idea was taken up again in 1896, when the first modern Olympics were held at Athens. The Games are now held every four years, each time in a different country, and many nations take part in the different sports. The winners receive gold, silver and bronze medals.

OPERA
An opera is a play in which the actors sing the words of the story. The first operas were written in Italy in the 1600s. The actors recited the story to music. Later, complete songs called arias were added. Many operas tell sad stories, but some are gay and have happy endings. Famous composers of operas include Monteverdi, Mozart, Verdi, Puccini and Wagner.

▲ **An oil rig** being towed out to oilfields in the North Sea.

ORCHESTRA
The word orchestra is used to describe any group of musicians, large or small, which plays together under a conductor.

▲ **A plan** of a symphony orchestra. About two-thirds of the musicians play stringed instruments.

There are various types: large symphony orchestras of about a hundred musicians, small chamber orchestras, orchestras with stringed instruments only, and theatre orchestras for musicals, ballets and opera.

The conductor directs and interprets the music, giving it its life and character. He indicates the speed, rhythm, expression and loudness of the music.

OSTRICH

The ostrich is the largest living bird. It has wings but cannot fly. Instead, it runs at great speed. Unlike other birds, the ostrich has only two toes.

Ostriches live in flocks on the dry African plains. They eat fruit, leaves and seeds and lay their eggs in the sand. In the past many ostriches were killed for their tail feathers, which were used to make fans and hats.

OTTER

Otters belong to the weasel family. They are wonderful swimmers. They paddle the water with their webbed toes and use their strong tails as rudders. Their thick fur keeps out the wet and cold. The river otter eats mostly fish and frogs. Its home is a hole in the river bank called a holt. The sea otter is larger and rarely comes on land.

OWL

Owls are birds of prey. Their large eyes see well in the dark and they fly noiselessly on their broad wings. Hunting by night, they swoop down on small animals such as mice and voles, and carry them off in their strong claws. The owl rips flesh with its hooked beak but it cannot digest fur, skin and bones. It spits them out in the form of a pellet.

OXYGEN

Oxygen, a colourless, odourless gas, is the commonest element on Earth. It combines easily with minerals and other substances. Oxygen is found in air, water and many different rocks.

All living things need oxygen. Animals need extra oxygen to move around and fire needs oxygen in order to burn. Plants give out oxygen in photosynthesis.

See also BREATHING; PHOTOSYNTHESIS.

▲ A mother otter with her cubs.

Eagle Owl

Brown form   Grey form

Tawny Owl

Short-eared Owl

FAMOUS PAINTERS

Giotto, Italian (*c.*1266–1337)
Jan van Eyck, Flemish
(*c.*1387–1440)
Sandro Botticelli, Italian
(*c.*1444–1510)
Leonardo da Vinci, Italian
(1452–1519)
Albrecht Durer, German
(1471–1528)
Michelangelo, Italian
(1475–1564)
Titian, Italian (1477–1576)
Raphael, Italian (1483–1520)
El Greco, Spanish
(*c.*1541–1614)
Rubens, Flemish (1577–1640)
Velasquez, Spanish
(*c.*1599–1666)
Rembrandt van Rijn, Dutch
(1606–1669)
Goya, Spanish (1746–1828)
J. M. W. Turner, English
(1775–1851)
Edouard Manet, French
(1832–1883)
Paul Cézanne, French
(1839–1906)
Henri Rousseau, French
(1844–1910)
Vincent van Gogh, Dutch
(1853–1890)
Vassily Kandinsky, Russian
(1866–1944)
Henri Matisse, French
(1869–1954)
Pablo Picasso, Spanish
(1881–1973)
Jackson Pollock, US
(1912–1956)

PAINTING

The oldest known paintings were made by Stone Age people in caves thousands of years ago. Much later, people started to decorate their homes and temples with paintings. Egyptians, Greeks, Romans and Chinese painted vases, pottery and walls.

During the Middle Ages in Europe most paintings were done for churches. So painters mostly painted stories from the Bible. Later Italian painters began to paint their Bible characters which looked like real people.

During the Renaissance painters often took scenes from history and Greek and Roman legends as their subjects. They also painted portraits of people from life, and realistic scenes from nature. During the 1700s many painters worked for fashionable society. They painted people in family groups, often against a background of a garden or a fine house.

Artists have always experimented with new ideas. 'Impressionist' painters, for instance, loved to paint light and shadow, and ignore the details, which could be captured perfectly in a photograph. By the early 1900s some were making pictures as designs and shapes, rather than as copies of objects. This is called *abstract* painting.

See also LEONARDO;
MICHELANGELO; PICASSO.

▲ **Raphael** is one of the most famous painters of the Renaissance. He painted many beautiful pictures of the Madonna and Child.

▲ *Light Red over Black*, an abstract painting by the American Mark Rothko (1950s).

▼ **A scene** of country life painted by the Flemish painter, Pieter Breughel in the 1500s.

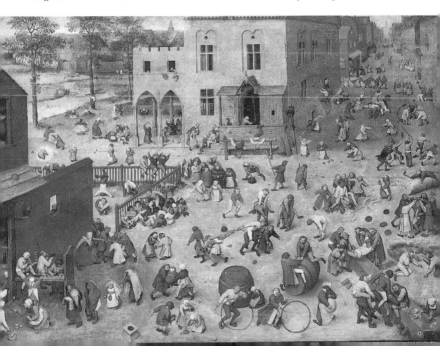

▲ **Pandas** are related to raccoons.

PANDA

One of the world's rarest animals is the giant panda. It looks like a furry black and white bear.

Pandas live in bamboo forests in the mountains of China. They eat mostly bamboo shoots and leaves. Pandas do not breed easily in captivity, so few have been seen in zoos outside China.

PAPER

The word paper comes from papyrus, the reed the Egyptians used to make paper. The type of paper we use today was invented by the Chinese about AD 105. It was made of mulberry bark. Small pieces of bark were soaked to separate the fibres, then dried into flat sheets. The use of paper spread after it was discovered by Arabs in the 700s.

With the invention of the printing press in the 1400s the demand for paper grew. In 1799 Louis Robert invented a machine to produce a continuous reel of paper. Today, most paper is made on machines from wood pulp obtained from tree fibres.

▼ **This diagram** shows how paper is made from timber. Logs are chopped into small pieces, then ground into pulp. The pulp is mixed with water and poured onto a wire mesh belt. The water drains away leaving a web of fibres which is dried and rolled.

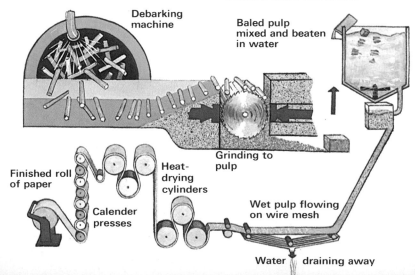

Debarking machine

Baled pulp mixed and beaten in water

Finished roll of paper

Heat-drying cylinders

Calender presses

Grinding to pulp

Wet pulp flowing on wire mesh

Water draining away

PARASITE

A parasite lives in or on some larger living thing and feeds on it. It is an uninvited guest. The animal or plant on which it lives is called a host.

Parasites often harm their hosts by taking too much food, or by causing diseases. Mistletoe (a plant), tapeworms, fleas, lice and mosquitoes (animals) are examples of parasites.

See also CUCKOO.

PARROT

A pet parrot may live up to fifty years and learn to 'talk'. Actually it only imitates sounds.

In the wild, parrots live in forests in Australia and other warm countries. They flock together high in the trees. The different kinds include parakeets, the cockatoos and macaws.

PASTEUR, Louis (1822–95)

Pasteur was a French scientist. He proved that bacteria and other germs cause diseases. Pasteur injectedweakened germs into animals and people to stop them catching the diseases those germs usually caused. He invented *pasteurization*: a way of heating milk and cooling it quickly to make it safe to drink. Pasteur also found out how tiny yeast cells turn sugar into alcohol.

PENGUIN

Penguins are sea birds that live on coasts around the Antarctic. Unable to fly, penguins use their wings as paddles and are excellent swimmers. They have a layer of thick fat to keep out the cold. Some kinds of penguins lay their eggs in rough nests on the rocks.

▲ **A West African** yellow-bellied parrot.

▲ **The Emperor penguin**'s chick sits on its parent's feet under a warm flap of feathers.

167

PENICILLIN

Penicillin is a kind of mould which, when processed, is used to stop the growth of many kinds of germs. It was the first antibiotic – a drug which kills bacteria.

PERFUME

Perfume is a fragrant essence in which more than a hundred natural aromatic (sweet-smelling or spicy) materials may be blended. The materials come from about 60,000 different flowers, leaves, fruits, seeds, woods, barks, resins and roots.

PERISCOPE

A periscope is an instrument used to see over walls and around corners. A simple periscope can be made from two mirrors, at a 45° angle, at either end of a tube. More complicated periscopes are used in submarines.

PHOTOGRAPHY

Photography was invented in 1839 by Louis Daguerre in France and William Fox Talbot in England.

Today there are cheap cameras which work automatically as well as the complex equipment, processes and techniques used by television and the cinema and in medical and scientific research.

See also CAMERA.

PHOTOSYNTHESIS

This is the process by which plants make food. Water from the soil and carbon dioxide gas from the air are combined to form sugars. This process can take place only in living plant cells which contain the green colouring matter, chlorophyll. The energy comes from sunlight.

See also LEAVES.

▲ **An early camera** called a *daguerreotype* after its inventor Louis Daguerre.

PICASSO, Pablo (1881–1973)

Picasso was a Spanish artist who greatly influenced art in this century. His painting changed from a realistic style to abstract styles like cubism which uses shapes such as cubes and triangles.

168

PIG

The pig is a very useful, intelligent animal. We eat its meat as pork, sausages, bacon and ham, its skin can be made into leather and its bristles go into brushes. Male pigs are called *boars*, and females *sows*. Pigs are unjustly accused of being dirty. They wallow in mud to keep themselves clean as well as cool.

PIRATE

Until about 150 years ago sea voyagers had more to fear than sudden storms. They faced the added danger of pirates. These fierce bands of sea-robbers sailed the seas in fast, well-armed ships. When they saw a merchant ship, they chased and captured it. They stole its cargo and robbed the passengers.

Some pirates became rich. Most were caught and hanged. By the 1800s ships could sail most seas without fear of pirates.

PLANET

Planets are small bodies which circle around the Sun. Unlike stars, planets do not produce their own light. They shine because they reflect the Sun's light. There are nine planets circling the Sun, Mercury (the planet nearest the Sun), Venus, Earth, Mars, Jupiter, Saturn, Uranus, Neptune and Pluto. There may be other planets beyond Pluto which have yet to be discovered. Jupiter is the largest planet — it is over 1000 times larger than the Earth. Mercury and Pluto are the smallest planets.

The planets can be divided into two groups, *gaseous* and *rocky*. The Earth is the biggest of the rocky planets, which also include Mercury, Venus, Mars and Pluto. Pictures taken by spacecraft have shown what the first three planets are like. They have a rough surface covered

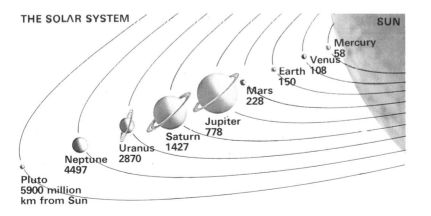

THE SOLAR SYSTEM

SUN

Mercury 58
Venus
Earth 108
150
Mars 228
Jupiter 778
Saturn 1427
Uranus 2870
Neptune 4497
Pluto 5900 million km from Sun

with great pits, or craters, and strewn with rocks. We know little about Pluto because it is so far away.

The other planets are made up mainly of gases. The giant planet Jupiter, for example, contains mostly hydrogen. Much of it is in very cold liquid form. The other gaseous planets are probably similar. Saturn and Neptune are surrounded by rings of gas and dust.

The Earth is the only planet known on which life can exist. Mercury and Venus are too hot for life to exist. And the outer planets are too cold. It is just possible that some kind of life could exist on Mars. But there are other planets in the Universe, circling around other suns.

PLANKTON
This is the drifting life of the sea. It is made up of tiny and microscopic plants and animals which float at or near the surface. Every sea animal depends in some way on plankton, because small fish feed on it and are eaten in turn by larger fish.

PLANT
There are more than 335,000 kinds of plant. Most plants are green. The green colour is caused by a substance called *chlorophyll*. This is used by the plant to make its food. The way it does this is called *photosynthesis*.

The plant kingdom includes several groups. The simplest plants of all are algae. Some algae are simply a single cell,

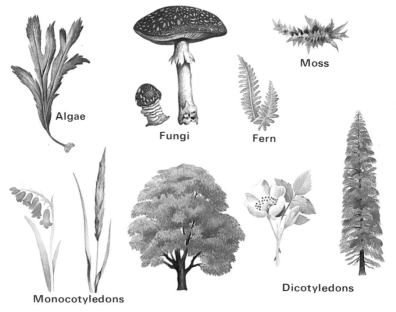

Algae

Fungi

Moss

Fern

Monocotyledons

Dicotyledons

which reproduces itself by splitting in two. Others, including seaweeds, are much bigger.

Fungi are plants which have no chlorophyll, so they are not green and cannot make their own food. Instead they feed on rotting or dead matter.

Mosses and liverworts are another group. They live on land. But, like fungi, they have no proper roots, and no flowers. Ferns are more advanced. They have stems, leaves and roots, but they cannot make flowers and seeds.

There are two sorts of flowering plants. *Monocotyledons*, such as lilies, bluebells, daffodils and grasses, have long straight leaves. *Dicotyledons*, such as peas, roses and broad-leaved trees, have broad leaves.

Seed-bearing plants produce male and female cells. The cells join to form a fertile seed which grows into a new plant.

See also ALGAE; FERN; FLOWER; GRASS; LEAVES; LICHEN; MUSHROOM AND TOADSTOOL; MOSS; PHOTOSYNTHESIS; SEAWEED; SEED; TREE.

PLASTICS

Plastics are man-made materials that have a wide variety of uses. They can be made into furniture, car bodies, clothing, and crockery. There are many different kinds of plastics, all of which can be shaped easily. Many are shaped by blowing, squirting or pressing into moulds.

Important plastics include nylon, polyethylene, PVC and polystyrene. All are made with chemicals obtained from oil. Some plastics are made from wood.

PLATYPUS

The curious platypus is a mammal that lays eggs. It lives in Australia. It has webbed feet, a tail like a beaver, thick fur and a duck-like bill. The platypus lives in a burrow in a river bank, and feeds under water on insects, worms and shellfish.

Platypus

PLAY

Plays were first performed in ancient Greece. Some were *tragedies*, plays that tell a serious story and often have sad endings. Others were *comedies*, plays with happy endings.

In the Middle Ages people performed *miracle* and *mystery* plays – stories from the Bible – or *morality* plays, in which the hero (main character) met a number of good and bad characters.

Some of the first indoor theatres were built in England in the 1500s. Companies of actors performed the plays of Shakespeare, Marlowe and Jonson. There was little scenery, and actors wore the clothes of their own day. Boys took women's parts, as women were not allowed to act.

Since the 1700s and 1800s plays have become closer to real life. They are written in simple, everyday language, and the plots (the stories) are usually about the lives of ordinary people.

FAMOUS PLAYWRIGHTS

Aeschylus, Greek (c.525–456 BC)
Sophocles, Greek (496–406 BC)
Euripedes, Greek (480–406 BC)
Aristophanes, Greek (c.450–406 BC)
William Shakespeare, English (1564–1616)
Ben Jonson, English (1572–1637)
Jean Baptiste Racine, French (1639–1699)
Richard Brinsley Sheridan, Irish (1751–1816)
Henrik Ibsen, Norwegian (1828–1906)
Oscar Wilde, Irish (1854–1900)
George Bernard Shaw, Irish (1856–1950)
Anton Chekhov, Russian (1860–1904)
Jean Cocteau, French (1889–1963)
Bertolt Brecht, German (1898–1956)
Samuel Beckett, Irish (born 1906)
Tennessee Williams, American (1911–1983)
Eugene Ionesco, French (born 1912)
Harold Pinter, English (born 1930)

POETRY

The oldest stories we know were first told as poetry. In a poem the words are often arranged to a musical beat or rhythm. Poetry which is written in a metre, or rhythm, is known as verse. But the rhythm does not have to be regular all the time. This would be dull. Blank verse has a rhythm, but it does not rhyme. Shakespeare used blank verse in his plays. Modern poets often prefer free verse, which does not rhyme or have a strict rhythm.

There are different styles and forms of poetry. Story poems with short verses and, often, with exciting stories are called *ballads*. Long story-poems are called *epics*. The greatest of the ancient epic poems, full of the deeds of brave heroes, are the *Iliad* and *Odyssey* of Homer, a Greek, and the *Aeneid* of the Roman poet Virgil.

Expressions of poets' feelings are called *lyrics*. They include such forms as the song, sonnet, ode, elegy and pastoral. Plays are sometimes written in poetry and these are called *dramatic* poems.

POISON

A poison is a substance which attacks the body, and can cause sickness or death. Some poisons are dangerous when swallowed. Others damage the lungs, the skin, and the nervous system. Chemicals, drugs, gases, acids and bad food can all be poisonous. Some medicines are also poisonous if used wrongly. So it is important always to follow the directions carefully.

▲ **Smoke** from factory chimneys pollutes the air.

POLAND

Poland is the seventh largest country in Europe. Most of its area is low-lying farmland where crops such as potatoes, wheat and flax are grown. In the south, there are also forests and mountains.

Coal mining is important in Poland and there are also many factories and industries in the big cities such as Warsaw, Gdansk, Poznan, Krakow and Wroclaw.

See also page 64.

▶ **The long spiny quills** on a porcupine's back are a good protection against enemies.

POLLUTION

Pollution is the contamination of soil, water or the atmosphere by harmful substances. Chemicals used to kill insects and weeds can build up and damage the soil. Sewage, waste from factories and oil from tankers pollute rivers and oceans. Smoke from chimneys and fumes from cars pollute the air.

Pollution can threaten our health, and even make it impossible for plants and animals to live. People are trying to find ways of preventing pollution.

POPE

The Pope is the head of the Roman Catholic Church and bishop of Rome. St Peter was the first bishop of Rome. The Pope lives in the Vatican, a tiny independent state in Rome. His chief advisers are the cardinals. They elect a new pope.

PORCUPINE

Porcupines are rodents. They live in forests and eat twigs, leaves and fruit. The porcupines of Africa and Asia live on the ground, but American porcupines are good climbers.

173

PORTUGAL

Portugal is the most westerly country of mainland Europe. The land varies from high plateaus in the north to lowlands with gentle hills and marshy plains in the south. The coast is low and sandy.

Many people work in agriculture or fishing. The chief crops are wheat, maize, fruit, grapes and olives. There are huge forests of cork oak.

See also page 64.

POST OFFICE

In early times messages were carried by runners or by riders on horseback. Fresh messengers and horses waited at 'posts', usually inns, along the road. Later, post coaches were used. The cost of delivering a letter was usually very expensive.

In 1840 a cheap postal system was started in Britain by Rowland Hill. For a standard charge of one penny (which bought a postage stamp) a letter was delivered anywhere in the country. See also STAMP.

POTATO

Potatoes are important food plants. The part you eat is a *tuber*, a swollen underground stem, in which the plant stores food. New plants grow from the 'eyes' in the tubers.

The potato plant grows wild in the Andes of South America. Explorers brought potatoes to Europe in the 1500s.

▶This chart shows how life developed in prehistoric times. A primitive form of life probably began in the Pre-Cambrian times, over 4,600 million years ago.

PREHISTORIC ANIMALS

The first animals appeared in the sea more than 700 million years ago. They may have been shaped as tiny blobs of jelly. Later some kinds developed protective shells. One common group, trilobites, looked like woodlice. All were invertebrates.

The first vertebrate animals (animals with backbones) were the fishes. which appeared about 450 million years ago. The first fishes had armoured bodies and heads.

At this time the land was still almost empty. There were plants and insect-like creatures but no vertebrates. Then, about 400 million years ago, some fishes crawled out of the water on to the land. They slowly developed legs instead of fins, and lungs with which they could breathe. They were the first amphibians.

Potato

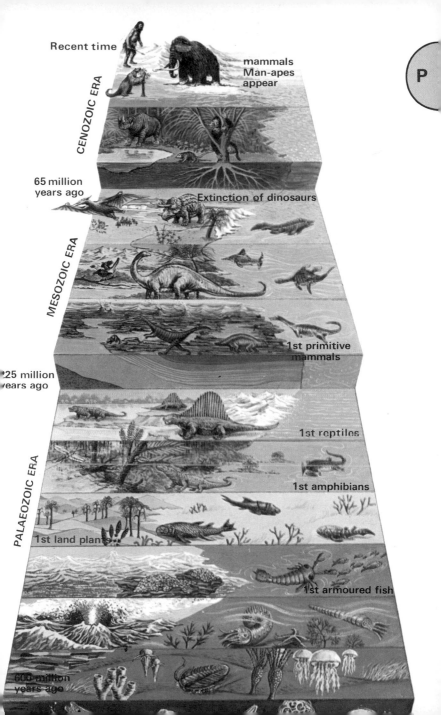

Recent time

mammals
Man-apes
appear

CENOZOIC ERA

65 million
years ago

Extinction of dinosaurs

MESOZOIC ERA

1st primitive
mammals

225 million
years ago

1st reptiles

1st amphibians

PALAEOZOIC ERA

1st land plants

1st armoured fish

600 million
years ago

Then came the reptiles. They adapted to different ways of life. Many were plant-eaters, but some were hunters, preying on other reptiles. About 200 million years ago some reptiles gave rise to dinosaurs. For millions of years dinosaurs ruled the Earth.

The first true birds may have evolved from dinosaurs which lived in trees and could just manage to glide from branch to branch.

The first mammals were small, insect-eating animals. For a long period of time they remained unimportant, while the dinosaurs ruled supreme. But when the dinosaurs died out, the little mammals took over and many different kinds developed. But many became extinct during the Ice Ages, when they were killed by a new mammal – man the hunter.

See also DINOSAUR; EVOLUTION; FOSSIL; ICE AGE; MAMMOTH.

▲ **Pages of a book** on a four-colour printing press.

PRESIDENT
France, Italy, the United States and many other countries all have a president. He or she is the head of state. The president is generally commander-in-chief of the army, navy and airforce. In the United States the president is also head of government like a prime minister.

PRIME MINISTER
A prime minister is a head of government. The prime minister usually leads the political party which has been voted the most seats in parliament. He or she chooses people called ministers to help run the government.

PRINTING
Before the 1400s, the usual way of producing books was to copy them by hand, so they were rare and expensive. Then, about 1450, Johannes Gutenberg made copies of the Bible on a printing press.

Gutenberg's method of printing was to build up his words from separate pieces of *type*, ink the type, then press paper against it. Printing by inking metal type (called *letterpress*) is still widely used. Many books are now printed by a photographic process (called *lithography*). The words are made up on a piece of film, and flat printing plates are made from the film. The plates are treated so that they pick up the ink only where the words are.

Photogravure, or *gravure*, is the reverse of the letterpress method. Letterpress prints from a raised plate; gravure from a recessed plate. Colour printing usually uses three colour printing plates as well as black. Most colours can be made by mixing three basic colours.

PYGMY
Pygmy men seldom grow much over 1·3 metres. One group of Pygmies live in the Congo basin in Africa.

African Pygmies are nomadic. They build simple shelters from the rain and use poison arrows to kill game.

PYRAMID
The ancient Egyptians buried their pharaohs (kings) in tombs called pyramids. They had four triangular sides meeting at the pointed top. Some are made of more than two million blocks of stone. Thousands of people dragged the huge stones slowly into place. Inside was a tomb where the *mummy* (preserved body) of the pharaoh was laid, surrounded by treasure. The best known pyramids are a group of three built at Giza about 2680–2565 BC.

▼ **Thousands** of people slaved to build the pyramids in Ancient Egypt.

177

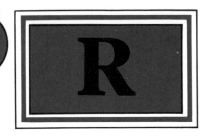

R

RABBIT AND HARE

Rabbits are burrowing animals. They live in colonies called warrens. Rabbits breed rapidly. There were none in Australia until the 1850s. Then a few English rabbits were set free. Soon there were rabbits everywhere.

Hares look like rabbits. But they are bigger, with longer ears and legs. Hares are swift runners. Unlike rabbits, they live alone, and do not dig burrows. Instead, they live in hollows called *forms*.

▼ **Rabbits** in their burrow.

RACCOON

The raccoon has long grey fur, a short pointed nose and a bushy tail tinged with black. Raccoons live in the Americas.

RADAR

Radar stands for *radio direction and ranging*. It is a device that can 'see' far away objects by bouncing radio waves off them. The waves travel like echoes back to the radar. They are picked up by the radar antennae and show up as small dots of light on a screen, rather like a television screen. From the position of the dot, the position of the object can be worked out. Ships and planes rely on radar for safety.

RADIO

Radio depends on radio waves. These invisible waves travel as fast as light waves. Radio works because radio waves can be made to carry signals which represent sound.

In a radio broadcasting studio sounds go into a microphone, where they are changed to electrical signals. These signals are combined with a 'carrier' wave, and transmitted by an aerial.

The aerial of a radio receiver picks up the carrier wave. Circuits in the receiver remove the carrier wave and leave only the electrical signals carrying the sound. These are fed to a loudspeaker which gives out the same sounds as went into the studio microphone.

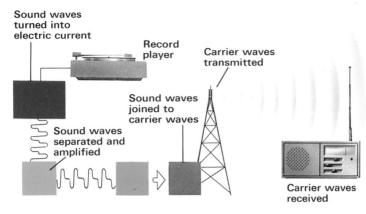

Sound waves turned into electric current

Record player

Carrier waves transmitted

Sound waves joined to carrier waves

Sound waves separated and amplified

Carrier waves received

RADIOACTIVITY

The atoms of most chemical elements do not change. But the atoms of some elements are unstable and emit (give out) atomic particles or radiation. We call this process radioactivity. Uranium and radium are radioactive elements.

See also ATOM; NUCLEAR ENERGY.

RAILWAY

The first public railway to use steam locomotives was the Stockton and Darlington line in the north of England. It was opened in 1825. George Stephenson, a self-taught engineer, built the ten-mile track and its first engine, called *Locomotion*. A few years later Stephenson built his

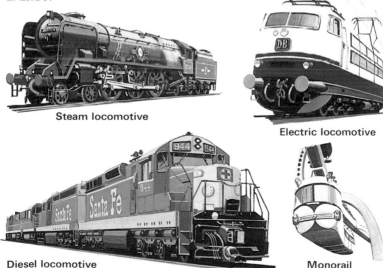

Steam locomotive

Electric locomotive

Diesel locomotive

Monorail

most famous locomotive, *The Rocket*. It was not long before people and goods could travel right across North America, Europe and Asia by rail.

Steam locomotives, belching smoke, hauled passenger trains and goods wagons for over one hundred years. But there are few left today. They have been replaced by diesel and electric locomotives which are cleaner, quieter and cheaper to run.

Until the beginning of this century the railways had no rivals. Then the motor car and the aeroplane were invented. Railways were used less and less and some lines closed. Now, new trains are in use which travel twice as fast as a car. And hover-trains which glide on a cushion of air have been invented.

RAIN

The rain comes from the water in seas, lakes, rivers and soil. The Sun's heat turns some of this water into water vapour which rises in the air. As the rising air cools, some of the water vapour 'condenses' or turns back to water droplets and becomes visible as clouds. As the air rises higher, more and more vapour turns back to water and the clouds grow bigger and darker. Finally, water droplets from the clouds fall to the ground as rain.

See also CLOUD.

RAT AND MOUSE

Rats and mice are rodents. They may eat and spoil our food, and also spread disease. Rats are bigger than mice. There are two main kinds: black and brown.

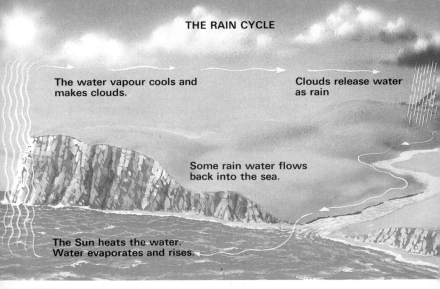

THE RAIN CYCLE

The water vapour cools and makes clouds.

Clouds release water as rain

Some rain water flows back into the sea.

The Sun heats the water. Water evaporates and rises.

Mice, like rats, breed quickly. The house mouse is a common pest. The wood mouse, the harvest mouse and the field mouse live in the country.

See also RODENT.

RECORDING

Modern records are discs of plastic which 'store' sound in their grooves. Another way of recording sound is on tape. Here, the sound is recorded in the form of a magnetic pattern. Television programmes can now be recorded on disc and tape. The sound track on films is often recorded as an image on the film.

See also VIDEOTAPE.

RED CROSS

The Red Cross organization helps the victims of wars and disasters. In 1859 the armies of France and Austria fought a terrible battle in Italy. A Swiss traveller, Jean Henri Dunant, saw thousands of wounded soldiers, who had been abandoned. He tried to help them, and wrote a book describing what he had seen. As a result, the Red Cross was formed at Geneva in Switzerland (a country which never takes part in war). Its flag is a red cross on a white background.

REFORMATION

This movement in the 1500s ended the religious unity of western Europe and led to the establishment of the Protestant Churches.

Until 1500 all Christians were Roman Catholics. Martin Luther, a German monk, disagreed with many of its teachings and protested in 1517. Many people agreed with him and a split developed. But not all Protestants believed the same things and so the movement itself split into the many types of Protestantism today.

See also PROTESTANT.

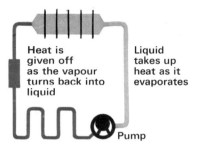

Heat is given off as the vapour turns back into liquid

Liquid takes up heat as it evaporates

Pump

▲ **Refrigerators** work on the principle that liquids absorb heat when they vaporize.

REFRIGERATION

Foods last longer when they are kept cool in a refrigerator. Cooling slows down the processes which make food go bad. Deep-freezers keep foods fresh by freezing them.

Refrigerators are worked by electricity or gas. They have a pump that turns a vapour into liquid. The liquid is turned into vapour again inside the freezing compartment. As it does so it takes up heat from the food. In another part of the refrigerator the vapour is changed back into a liquid and recirculated.

RELIGION

A religion is a belief, a way of living, or both. It may mean belief in a god or gods with powers greater than our own, and in another life after this one. It may involve prayer and worship.

All the world's great religions began in Asia. The oldest religion to teach that there is only one god is *Judaism*, the religion of the Jews. Its history is told in the Hebrew Bible, which Christians call the Old Testament.

The followers of *Islam* are called Muslims. Muslims believe in Allah, the one god, and obey the teachings of the Koran, their holy book.

Hinduism is the chief religion of India. Hindus believe people's souls are reborn many times until they are good enough to join Brahma, a supreme power.

Buddhism is another important Eastern religion. Its founder, Buddha ('The Enlightened One'), taught people how to escape from suffering and find peace.

People who follow the teachings of Jesus Christ are *Christians*.

Other important world religions are Confucianism, Taoism, Zoroastrianism, Shintoism and Sikhism.

See also BIBLE; BUDDHA; HINDUS; JESUS CHRIST; JEWS; MAGIC; MUHAMMAD; PROTESTANTS; KORAN.

▲ **Rembrandt** was an old man when he painted this self-portrait around 1660.

REMBRANDT VAN RIJN
(1606–69)

Rembrandt was a Dutch artist who has become one of the most famous painters in the world. He was a master in the use of light, colour and mood. His most famous paintings are portraits.

RENAISSANCE

In the 1300s there began a rebirth of learning in Europe. Scholars rediscovered and studied the ancient writings of Greece and Rome. Artists such as Leonardo da Vinci and Michelangelo recaptured the beauty of 'classical' Greek architecture and sculpture. Scientists such as Copernicus and Galileo questioned the old ideas about the Universe. Explorers brought back new knowledge from their voyages. 'Humanist' thinkers taught that human beings were not just weak creatures ruled by God.

182

REPRODUCTION

All animals and plants can reproduce. Simple animals and plants can reproduce on their own. They either divide in two (like the amoeba) or make special cells which grow into new plants (like the fungi).

More advanced forms of life reproduce sexually by producing special sex cells. When a male cell joins with and fertilizes a female cell, this grows into a new individual. In flowering plants a

REPTILE

Reptiles are cold-blooded animals – their body temperature is the same as the temperature of their surroundings. Because of this reptiles cannot live in very cold lands. In places where there are cold winters, they hibernate.

Reptiles have tough, scaly skins and most lay leathery-shelled eggs. Baby reptiles hatch fully developed and are not cared for by their parents.

There are four main groups of

▲ **The chameleon** is a reptile. It can change its colour to match its background.

male sex cell stored in a pollen grain joins a female sex cell in the carpel. In animals, the male cells are called sperms, and the female cells, eggs.

See also CELL; ANIMAL; FLOWER; GENETICS; HUMAN BODY.

reptiles: alligators and crocodiles, snakes and lizards, tortoises and turtles and the very rare tuatara. Most eat insects and small animals, but some eat plants.

See also CROCODILE AND ALLIGATOR; DINOSAUR; LIZARD; SNAKE; TORTOISE AND TURTLE.

REVOLUTION

The word *revolution* means 'turn around' or 'complete change'. If a country has a revolution, its government and laws are overthrown, often by war and bloodshed.

The most famous revolutions in history happened in America, France and Russia. In 1776 the American colonies broke away from Britain and became an independent republic. The French Revolution, 1789, caused the overthrow of the king and the nobles who ruled France. In 1917 the rule of the Russian Tsar was ended, and the world's first Communist government was set up.

Another kind of revolution is economic. It changes the way people live.

RHINOCEROS

The rhinoceros is the second largest land animal, after the elephant. The black rhinoceros and the white rhinoceros live on the African plains. Actually, both are grey. The rhinoceroses of India, Java and Sumatra live in dense forests. Rhinoceroses eat grass, shoots and twigs.

RIVER

Rivers begin their lives as small streams in hills or mountains. Some begin as trickles of water from melting glaciers. Others bubble up through the ground as springs.

Gravity makes water flow downhill. At first the river rushes along, fed by rain and melting snow. It is narrow but fast-flowing, forming rapids and waterfalls, and carrying along with it stones which help to deepen and widen its course.

▼ **Two black rhinos** in Tanzania.

When it reaches flatter country, the river flows more slowly. Other streams, called tributaries, may join it. The river valley gradually becomes wider and flatter and it meanders or loops from side to side. Finally, the river flows into the sea, sometimes through a fan-shaped network of channels known as a delta. The fresh water of many a river meets the salt water of the sea in a river mouth, or estuary.

See also WATER.

ROAD

Roads are made up of layers. Tarmac roads have layers of tar and stones on top of well-rammed soil. Concrete roads are made up of layers of concrete.

John McAdam was a pioneer roadmaker in the 1800s and Italians built the first modern motorway in the 1920s. Two thousand years before, their ancestors, the Romans, were building fine roads throughout Europe, North Africa and the Middle East.

ROBOT

The word robot comes from a Czech play about mechanical people. The Czech word 'robota' means work or worker. In films and books set in the future robots often look like metal people and they can walk, talk and think.

Real robots are very different. They are machines with arms that can move in several directions. Robots are *programmable* machines. This means they can be instructed to carry out different tasks. The instructions or programs are stored in the robot's computer brain.

Most robots work in industry and do jobs such as paint spraying, welding and heavy lifting and loading. Some robots work in places which are dan-

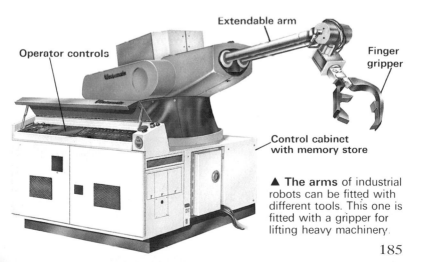

Extendable arm

Operator controls

Finger gripper

Control cabinet with memory store

▲ **The arms** of industrial robots can be fitted with different tools. This one is fitted with a gripper for lifting heavy machinery.

185

gerous for humans such as nuclear power stations and outer space.

See also COMPUTER.

ROCK

The inside of the Earth is a hot, molten mass. But the outer skin, or crust, is made up of solid rock. All rocks belong to three great groups: the *igneous*, the *sedimentary* and the *metamorphic*. All igneous rocks were once molten (melted) and came from deep in the Earth. Sedimentary rocks are formed of layers of materials such as sand and clay which have been cemented together under pressure. Metamorphic rocks have been changed from their original form to another by heat and pressure.

ROCKET

A rocket is a kind of engine. It works by shooting out a stream of gases backwards. As the gases go backwards the rocket goes forward. The rocket works rather like a jet engine. Both burn fuel to make hot gases, which shoot out in a stream. But the rocket carries its own oxygen to burn the fuel. The jet engine gets its oxygen from the air.

See also JET ENGINE.

RODENT

Rodents are mammals that have chisel-like front teeth which are specially adapted for gnawing. There are more than 6000 species of rodent – more than any other

▲ **The powerful space rocket** Apollo 2 at take-off.

kind of mammal. Beavers, squirrels, gophers, hamsters, gerbils and porcupines are all rodents. They are found everywhere. The smallest rodent is the mouse. The largest is the capybara which is the shape and size of a pig.

Rodents have many enemies. They are preyed on by hawks, owls, snakes, foxes and other animals.

See also BEAVER; GUINEA PIG; PORCUPINE; RAT AND MOUSE; SQUIRREL.

186

ROME, ANCIENT

According to legend, Rome was founded by twin brothers called Romulus and Remus, who were raised by a she-wolf. At first the Romans were ruled by foreign kings. But in 509 BC the people set up a republic in which they elected their own rulers. They fought against their neighbours and built a powerful army. In 217 BC the first emperor took power.

Without their army, the Romans would never have conquered and ruled their Empire, which eventually stretched from Britain to the Middle East.

The Roman Empire was divided into provinces, ruled by governors. The capital of the Empire was the city of Rome, built on seven hills. To the Romans, Rome was the centre of the world. At the height of its power, Rome was a city of great splendour.

In AD 295 the Empire was divided into two. One half was ruled from Rome, the other from Byzantium (Constantinople). Rome was no longer strong. Its government was dishonest, and the army could no longer fight off the barbarian raids. Around AD 476 the western empire fell, and Rome was destroyed. In the east, the Byzantine Empire lasted until 1453 when Constantinople was captured by the Turks.

See also BYZANTINE EMPIRE; CAESAR; HANNIBAL.

▶ The Romans were great civil engineers. Here is an aqueduct being built.

RUBBER

Rubber trees grow in tropical countries such as Malaysia and Indonesia. To make rubber, cuts are made in the bark of the tree and a milky sap (latex) oozes out, which is treated with acid to produce crude rubber. Other things are mixed with it, and then it is moulded to make soles of shoes, tyres, tubes and many other things. Much of the rubber used now, however, is made by the plastics industry.

RUTHERFORD, Ernest
(1871–1937)

Rutherford was a New Zealand-born British physicist. He was a pioneer of atomic science and his main research was in the field of radioactivity. Rutherford was the first to 'split' the atom. He received the Nobel chemistry prize in 1914.

▼ **This Malaysian woman** is tapping latex from a rubber tree.

SAINT

A saint is a holy person whom Christians believe came close to being perfect. Some saints, like St Francis of Assisi, are remembered for their good lives. Others, such as St Bernadette of Lourdes, are believed to perform miracles of healing.

To become a saint a person must be *canonized* with the approval of the Roman Catholic Church. A commission is set up by the Church to examine carefully everything known about the person's life.

SALT

Salts make up a class of chemicals. There are many different salts, but the one we know best is the salt we eat – common salt. It is made up of the two elements sodium and chlorine. Our bodies need salt. There is salt in blood, sweat and in tears.

SATELLITE

A satellite is a small body which circles around a larger one. The Moon is the Earth's satellite. It circles the Earth once a month. Most planets have satellites. We often just call them moons.

The Earth now has many man-made satellites circling around it. The first artificial satellite, called *Sputnik I*, was launched by the Russians in 1957. To resist Earth's gravity a satellite must speed round at 28,000 kilometres an hour. Satellites can be very useful. Some help in weather forecasting. Some relay telephone and television all over the world.

SCANDINAVIA

This is a region in northern Europe. It includes the countries of Norway, Sweden, Denmark, Iceland and Finland. History and trade have brought them close together.

The Scandinavian Peninsula is a long strip of land, surrounded by cold seas. There are high mountains, and on the west coast are long, narrow inlets called *fiords*. The northern part of Scandinavia is inside the Arctic Circle. The people who live there are the Lapps. The forests of Scandinavia produce timber. Farming and fishing are important occupations.

See also VIKINGS and page 64.

SCIENCE

The word 'science' just means knowledge. In science, people try to find out about the world around them by observing things

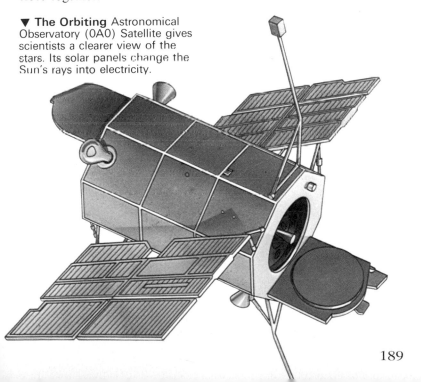

▼ **The Orbiting** Astronomical Observatory (OAO) Satellite gives scientists a clearer view of the stars. Its solar panels change the Sun's rays into electricity.

and carrying out experiments. Scientists try to classify new facts, and fit them in with what they know already.

Chemistry, physics and biology are the main branches of science. Chemistry studies the way matter is made up. Physics studies the properties of matter and energy, and biology studies living things.

See also CHEMISTRY; ZOOLOGY.

SCOUTS AND GUIDES
The scout movement for boys was started in 1908 by a British soldier, Robert Baden-Powell. Girl guides began in 1910. Scouts and guides try to help other people and each other. There are more than 17 million scouts and guides in the world.

SCULPTURE
Making models and figures, or statues, is a form of art called sculpture. Sculpture is done in two ways: by *carving* and *moulding*. In carving, the sculptor cuts into a block of wood or stone with sharp tools. In moulding, he makes a model in soft clay, then bakes the clay to harden it. From the hard model he makes a mould, and pours into it wet concrete or hot, liquid metal (such as bronze). When this hardens, a perfect 'casting' of the model is left.

Today sculptors also use materials such as pieces of glass, metal and cloth, as well as wood and stone.

Sea horse

SEA HORSE
The sea horse is actually a small sea fish. It gets its name from its horse-like head. The sea horse swims in a curious upright position, fanning its dorsal (back) fin. It can cling on to seaweed, using its coiled tail.

▼ **A bronze figure** of a cock by the painter and sculptor Pablo Picasso.

190

SEALS AND SEA LIONS

These mammals spend most of their time in the sea. Their legs have become flippers, and they are expert swimmers, but they have to come to the surface to breathe. Seals and sea lions catch fish underwater. Seals swim by moving their bodies from side to side. Sea lions use their front flippers like oars.

These animals come ashore to breed. They gather in large colonies on rocky coasts. Seals are slow and clumsy on land. But sea lions can turn their back flippers forwards and move quite quickly.

SEASONS

The different times of the year are called seasons. They are caused by the way the Earth orbits, or travels round, the Sun. When the North Pole leans towards the Sun, northern lands have their summer and southern lands their winter. At the opposite point of the orbit, when the North Pole leans away from the Sun, northern lands have their winter and southern lands their summer. Spring and autumn are the points in the orbit when the Equator, at the middle of the Earth, faces the Sun, so northern and southern lands have roughly the same amount of warmth.

SEAWEED

Seaweeds are simple plants of the algae group. They do not have flowers or proper roots. Green seaweed grows high up the beach. Brown seaweed grows lower down, while red seaweed lives in deeper water. Seaweeds need sunlight, so none grows deeper than about 75 metres.

Some seaweeds can be eaten. Other kinds are used to make good fertilizers.

THE SEASONS

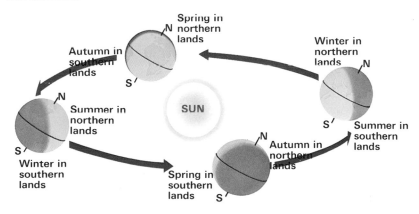

SEVEN WONDERS OF THE WORLD

1 *The Pyramids of Egypt.* 2 *The Lighthouse of Pharos at Alexandria.* 3 *The Colossus of Rhodes.* 4 *The Statue of Zeus at Olympia.* 5 *The Hanging Gardens of Babylon.* 6 *The Temple of Artemis.* 7 *The Mausoleum at Halicarnassus.*

SEED

Most plants reproduce themselves by means of seeds. They are formed in the plant's ovary. A seed contains an *embryo* – the plant in its earliest form. Seeds lie dormant or asleep until conditions are right for them to *germinate*. To germinate they need moisture, warmth, air and darkness.

SENSES

Senses tell us what is happening around us and inside us. We have external senses of hearing, taste, touch, sight and smell. Each sense comes from nerve endings or sense organs which send signals to our brain along the nervous system. For example, nerve endings on our tongue, called taste buds, tell us whether food is salty, sour, sweet or bitter. Internal senses tell us when we are hungry, tired or thirsty. And our muscle sense tells us the position of different parts of our body.

SEVEN WONDERS OF THE WORLD

Travellers in ancient times marvelled at the Seven Wonders of the World. Of these wonders only the Pyramids can still be seen. The others (illustrated left) have been destroyed.

SHAKESPEARE, William
(1564–1616)

Shakespeare is often called the world's greatest writer. He was born in Stratford on Avon. His plays are written in some of the most beautiful poetry in the English language. Some like *Richard II* and *Richard III* are about history. Others, like *A Midsummer Night's Dream*, are comedies. *Hamlet*, *Macbeth*, *Othello* and *King Lear* are great tragedies.

SHARK

Sharks are the most feared hunters of the sea. Drawn by the smell of blood, they will kill fish, seals, porpoises and even whales. Some sharks are man-eaters, but most kinds are harmless.

Sharks are strong, fast-swimming fish. Their gaping jaws are full of sharp teeth. Instead of bones, sharks have gristly skeletons.

▼ **Sharks** have rough skin like sandpaper.

SHEEP

Sheep are important farm animals. We make their wool into cloth, eat their meat and wear their skins. Sheep are easy to keep. They can feed on rough pasture, and their thick coats

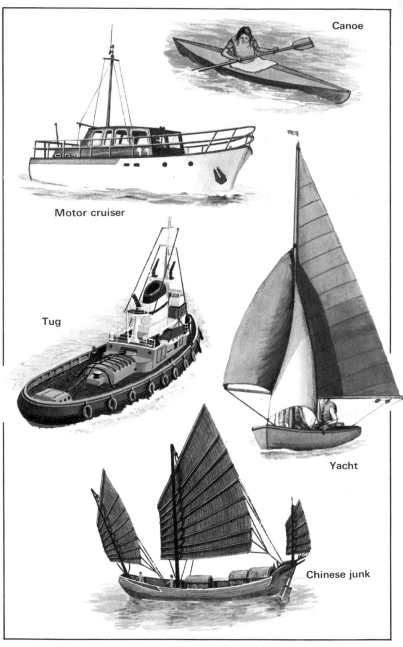

S

Canoe

Motor cruiser

Tug

Yacht

Chinese junk

keep out bad weather. Wild sheep live in the mountains in parts of America, Europe and Asia.

SHIP

For at least 4000 years ships have been sailing across seas. They still transport most of the world's cargo between the continents, but few carry passengers.

Until about a hundred years ago most ships were propelled by sails. For many years ships had only one square sail on a single mast. They could only sail well with the wind and relied on oars to propel them at other times. The Viking longships were an example of this.

By the 1400s ships were built with several masts, one of which carried a triangular sail which made sailing easier in all winds. Soon came the three-masted caravels and galleons. Last of the sailing ships were the graceful and speedy clippers, which carried wool or tea from Australia or the Far East.

See also SUBMARINE.

SILICON CHIP

Silicon is the most common element after oxygen in the Earth's crust. Silicon chips are tiny pieces of silicon – as small as one square millimetre – made to carry minute electrical circuits which are used in digital watches, electronic calculators and computers and transistor radios.

See also COMPUTER.

SILK

The beautiful smooth cloth called silk is made from threads spun by the silkworm. This is actually the caterpillar of a moth. When the caterpillar is fully grown, it wraps itself in a cocoon of fine silk, stuck together with gum. The ancient Chinese were the first to discover how to wash away the gum and unwind the silk on to reels. It was then dyed and woven into cloth.

SILVER

Silver is a beautiful shiny metal which is used to make jewellery and expensive tableware. It can be shaped easily by bending and hammering.

Silver is interesting to the scientist because it conducts (passes on) heat and electricity better than any other substance. It also forms compounds that are sensitive to light. They are used in photography.

▲ **A silicon chip** mounted in a plastic carrier is shown next to an apple.

SKIING

Skiing has been the main way of getting about on deep snow for thousands of years. Skis from about 3000 BC have been found in Sweden. It is only during the last hundred years that skiing has been enjoyed as a sport. Ski racing and ski jumping were developed in Scandinavia about 1860. Downhill and slalom races are also international competitions.

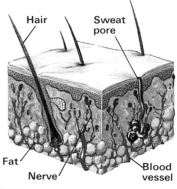

SKIN

Skin is more than just the covering of the body. It helps prevent us getting too hot or too cold. It helps keep out harmful germs. And it helps the body get rid of waste.

The skin is in two layers. The outer layer is the *epidermis*. It grows all the time, to replace dead skin cells which are rubbed off.

Underneath the epidermis is a thicker layer called the *dermis*. It contains nerves and blood vessels. Hair grows out of it. The sweat glands are here too.

SKUNK

Skunks live in North America. They are relatives of badgers and weasels, and are animals of the woodlands. They eat insects, birds' eggs and small mammals. If attacked, the skunk turns its back, raises its bushy tail, and squirts out a foul-smelling spray of liquid from a special gland.

SLAVERY

Slavery means owning people. Slaves can be bought and sold as workers. They were often forced to do hard, cruel work and many died because their owners treated them badly. In ancient Egypt, Greece and Rome there were a great many slaves.

When Europeans began settling in America, they took Negro slaves from Africa to work on the plantations. This slave trade was not stopped until the 1800s. All the Negro slaves in the southern United States were freed in 1865 after the American Civil War.

SLEEP AND DREAMS

We spend about a third of our lives asleep. Our minds and bodies do not stop working while we sleep, but they do slow down. Without sleep, we feel tired and cross, and we cannot concentrate.

Part of the brain is active during sleep. Though our eyelids are closed, our eyes move rapidly. When this happens, scientists know we are dreaming.

SLOTH

In the South American forest lives the slow-moving sloth. This strange mammal spends its life hanging upside down in trees. It eats leaves and fruit. The sloth's hooked claws are good for climbing, but useless for walking on the ground. The hair of the sloth hangs downwards, so rainwater runs off easily. Sometimes algae grow on the hair, helping to hide the sloth from enemies such as the jaguar.

▲ **Sloths** sleep most of the day.

SLUG AND SNAIL

Slugs and snails are molluscs but slugs have little or no shell. They both like dark, cool places and die if they get too dry or hot. Slugs and snails are garden pests, eating young and low-lying plants. Some varieties eat worms and other molluscs.

See also MOLLUSC.

SNAKE

Snakes are legless reptiles. Unlike lizards, snakes have no eyelids. Most snakes lay eggs, but some give birth to live young.

All snakes prey on other animals, such as insects, birds, frogs and small mammals. Poisonous snakes kill their prey by biting it with their fangs and

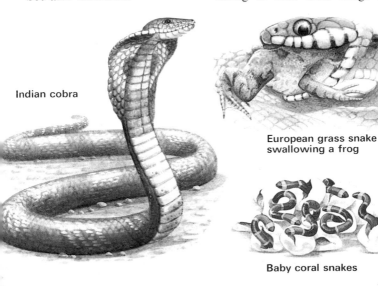

Indian cobra

European grass snake swallowing a frog

Baby coral snakes

197

injecting poison, or 'venom', into its body. Many snakes have no poison but grab their prey with their sharp teeth. Some large snakes, like the python, coil their long bodies around their prey and crush it until it suffocates.

There are some 2500 different kinds of snakes, of which only about 150 are dangerous to humans.

See also REPTILE.

SNOW
Inside a cloud are millions of tiny water droplets. At the top, where the air is coldest, the water freezes to ice. Sometimes the drops of ice melt as they pass into warmer air and they fall as rain. But if the air is cold enough, they fall as snowflakes.

Snowflakes are tiny crystals. Each one has a beautiful pattern and always has six sides. A large snowflake is made of thousands of crystals stuck together.

SOAP
Soap is a substance which helps wash away dirt and grease. The tiny soap particles are able to stick to and surround specks of dirt, and float them away in the water. Soap is made by boiling animal or vegetable fat with a chemical called an alkali.

Chemical cleaners called *detergents* are often used today instead of soap.

SOIL
A handful of garden soil does not look very interesting. But it is alive with millions of tiny plants and animals which help to keep soil fertile.

Soil is made from crumbled rocks. The process of wearing down rocks into small pieces takes millions of years. When plants and animals die, their remains are broken down by bacteria into 'humus'. Humus holds moisture in the soil and binds the soil together. Fertile soil holds a lot of water and air.

SOUND
Sound is produced by objects that are vibrating to and fro. If you touch the strings of a violin, you can feel them vibrating. A

◄ **Children** playing in the snow.

vibrating string gently nudges the molecules of the air as it goes to and fro. These air molecules nudge other air molecules and a wave spreads from the string through the air, just as ripples spread on a pond.

When the sound wave strikes our ears, it causes our eardrums to vibrate and nerves send signals to the brain. This is how we hear. If there were no air, there would be nothing to carry the sound. That is why there is no sound in space.

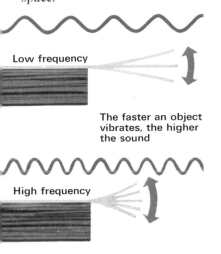

Low frequency

The faster an object vibrates, the higher the sound

High frequency

Sounds are described in various ways. They can be loud or soft; high or low. High sounds, or, rather, high-pitched sounds, are made by things that vibrate rapidly. Low-pitched sounds are made by slow vibrations.

Some things produce sound waves pitched too high for us to hear. We call these waves *ultrasonic*.

SOUTH AFRICA

The Republic of South Africa lies at the southern end of Africa. It is a warm, sunny land and many wild animals roam in its huge national parks. But there are also large cities, such as Johannesburg, Cape Town and Durban. South Africa is a rich country. Farming and mining (for gold, diamonds and uranium) are the chief activities.

Although most South Africans are black, Coloured (of mixed race) or Asian, the whites control the government. The whites live separately too, part of a policy called *apartheid* or 'separate development'.

See also page 64.

SOUTH AMERICA

There are 13 countries in South America. At 17,600,000 square kilometres, it is the fourth largest continent in the world. It has dense rain forests, barren deserts, wide grasslands and high mountains.

The Andes Mountains, the highest in all South America, stretch for over 7000 kilometres down the western side, overlooking the Pacific Ocean. In the centre of the continent are vast plains. They include the forests of the Amazon basin which cover an area the size of Western Europe, the endless swamps and lakes of the Gran Chaco, and the grassy pampas of Argentina.

South America is rich in minerals, such as copper, tin,

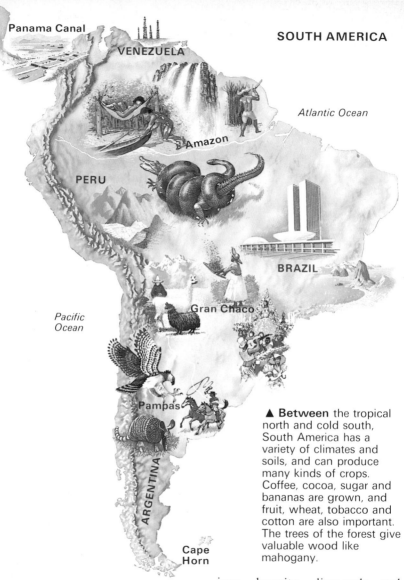

Panama Canal

VENEZUELA

SOUTH AMERICA

Atlantic Ocean

Amazon

PERU

BRAZIL

Pacific Ocean

Gran Chaco

Pampas

ARGENTINA

Cape Horn

▲ **Between** the tropical north and cold south, South America has a variety of climates and soils, and can produce many kinds of crops. Coffee, cocoa, sugar and bananas are grown, and fruit, wheat, tobacco and cotton are also important. The trees of the forest give valuable wood like mahogany.

iron, bauxite, diamonds and emeralds. Mining is an important industry everywhere, and there are also large oilfields, particularly off the coast of Venezuela.

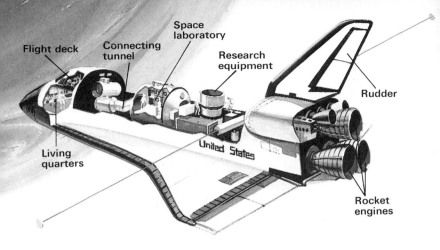

Flight deck
Connecting tunnel
Space laboratory
Research equipment
Rudder
Living quarters
United States
Rocket engines

▲ **The Space Shuttle Columbia** is launched by rockets, orbits like a spacecraft and can land back on Earth like an airliner.

Today, South America is a rapidly changing continent. Its governments are sometimes democratic, but more often are controlled by military leaders.

See also ARGENTINA; BRAZIL; INCAS and page 65.

SPACE FLIGHT

The Russians launched the first spacecraft, *Sputnik I* in October 1957. The first man went into space in April 1961 when the Russian Yuri Gagarin flew once around the Earth. The first woman in space in 1963, was also a Russian. The Americans put the first men on the Moon in July 1969.

Today, many spacecraft are being sent into space. Some, like

satellites and probes, are unmanned. Satellites carry equipment such as measuring instruments, tape recorders, radios and cameras. Probes are sent to explore the Moon and planets. Probes have already photographed all the planets out to Saturn, and have landed on Venus and Mars.

See also ASTRONAUT; SATELLITE.

SPAIN

Spain is in south-western Europe. Much of the centre of the country is a high plateau, where few trees grow. Northern Spain is wet and cool, but the south is hot and dry.

Most Spanish people work on farms. Spain is famous for olives, oranges and onions. Important industries are textiles, steelmaking and engineering. Many tourists visit Spain every year.

In the late 15th century, Spain became rich and strong and built up a huge empire, mainly in South America. Later, however, Spain grew weak and lost its overseas lands.

In 1931 Spain became a republic. From 1936 to 1939 there was a terrible civil war, after which General Franco ruled as a dictator. When he died in 1975 Spain became a kingdom again.

SPINNING AND WEAVING
Spinning is the process of twisting man-made or natural fibres into threads by hand or using machinery.

The commonest means of joining the yarns together to make a fabric is called weaving. Weaving is done on a loom. In weaving, one set of yarns (the *weft*) is threaded at right angles under and over another set (the *warp*). The warp yarns run lengthways.

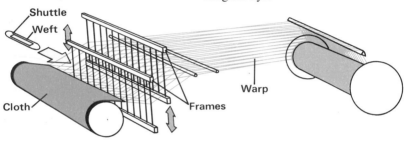

▲ **The shuttle** carries the weft threads back and forth across the warp on a weaving loom.

SPIDER
Spiders may look like insects but they are not. Their bodies are made up of two parts (not three) and they have eight legs (not six). They are related to scorpions.

All spiders make silk inside their bodies. Some spiders use the silk to make webs to trap insects for food. However, not all spiders build webs. Wolf spiders chase their prey on the ground. Crab spiders lurk inside flowers, while trapdoor spiders lie in wait in holes.

▼ **The trapdoor spider** hides in a hole and waits for its prey to pass. It then leaps out and grabs the creature.

▲ **Red squirrels** are rare in Britain today.

SQUIRREL

Squirrels are small furry animals with bushy tails. They belong to the rodent family. Most squirrels live in trees. The red squirrel lives in Europe and Asia. The North American grey squirrel has spread to other countries.

Some squirrels live in holes in the ground. Gophers, prairie dogs and chipmunks are ground squirrels which live in America.

See also RODENT.

STALACTITE AND STALAGMITE

These are two types of mineral deposits found in caves. Stalactites grow downward from the roof. Stalagmites grow up from the floor and can be as much as 30 metres high.

Both types are formed by water that seeps into the caves and drips from the limestone ceilings. The water is often saturated with dissolved minerals that are deposited in icicle like formations. They are sometimes called dripstones.

See also CAVE.

STALIN, Joseph (1879–1953)

Stalin was a revolutionary leader who worked to overthrow the Tzar of Russia in 1917. As leader of the Soviet Union from 1924 to his death, he helped to turn Russia into an industrialized state. But Stalin was responsible for millions of deaths, and in 1959 he was denounced as a dictator.

STAMP

Postage stamps were first used in Britain in 1840. They were the idea of a man called Rowland Hill. The first British stamps were a penny black and a twopenny blue. To stop stamps being used twice, the post office 'cancels' them with an ink postmark. This shows where and when the letter was posted.

See also POST OFFICE.

203

STAR

The stars we see in the night sky are balls of glowing gases. They are so far away that they seem very tiny, but if we could get closer, they would look like the Sun. The Sun is a star, and a very ordinary one. Some stars are much bigger and brighter than the Sun; others much smaller and dimmer. Stars shine by nuclear power: heat and light produced when atoms of hydrogen gas fuse, or join together.

▲ **The great cluster** in Hercules may contain half a million stars.

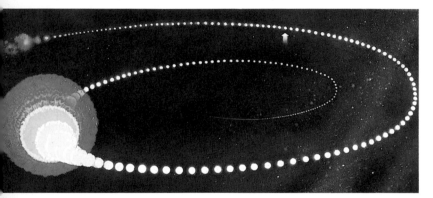

▲ **The life and** death of a star. Stars form from gases. They shine steadily for a long time, then expand into *red giants*. Finally they die away as tiny *white dwarfs*.

Astronomers are not sure how stars originated but many think that they are formed out of great clouds of cool dust and gases.

See also NUCLEAR POWER; SUN; UNIVERSE.

STEAM ENGINE

James Watt built the first really efficient steam engines in the late 1700s and made them suitable for driving industrial machinery of all kinds.

In Watt's type of engine, steam pushes a piston back and forth in a cylinder. The piston is connected to whatever is to be driven – for example, the wheels of a locomotive. Steam is produced by burning coal or wood in a furnace beneath a boiler. The hot gases from the furnace pass through tubes in the boiler and heat the water. The steam which is produced drives the pistons.

STONE AGE

This is the name given to the period before people learned to obtain and use metal. Tools and weapons were made from flint and other rocks and wood. The Stone Age probably began about three million years ago.

There are three Stone Age periods: the Old (Palaeolithic), Middle (Mesolithic) and New (Neolithic).

At the beginning of the Old Stone Age, hunters made clumsy stone axes. Thousands of years were to pass before they could chip flint into double-edged blades with which they made more effective implements: knives, scrapers and weapons.

Middle Stone Age people made more intricate tools and weapons. Many were set in wooden or bone hafts and handles, making them easier to use.

Farming replaced hunting in the New Stone Age. Tools became more refined and more specialized for a particular task.

See also BRONZE AGE; IRON AGE.

SUBMARINE

Ships that can travel under water are called submarines. A submarine dives by letting water into tanks around the hull (body). This makes it heavier than water. To surface, it blows the water out, making it lighter again. A periscope enables the captain to see above the surface.

Ordinary submarines are propelled under water by a propeller driven by electric batteries. They

▼ **James Watt** built this steam engine in 1788. The steam drove pistons connected to a beam. As the beam rocked, gears turned a drive wheel.

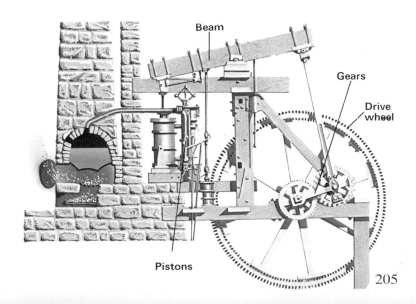

Beam

Gears

Drive wheel

Pistons

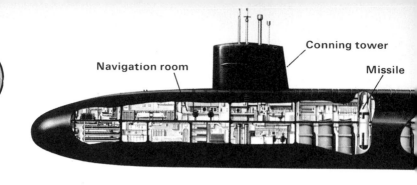

Navigation room

Conning tower

Missile

▲ **This cutaway** drawing of a nuclear submarine shows the navigation room beneath the conning tower and the nuclear reactor and steam turbine engine in the stern.

have to surface when their batteries run down. On the water they are propelled by diesel engines, which also charge the batteries. Nuclear submarines are powered by a nuclear reactor. They can remain under water for months at a time.

SUGAR
Plants make sugar for their own food. The sugar that we use to sweeten food is called *sucrose*. It comes from sugar beet and sugar cane. Other sugars are *fructose* (from fruits), *glucose* (from fruits, vegetables and grain), and *lactose* (from milk).

Sugar is a very important food because it supplies energy and heat and helps to form fat.

SUN
The Sun is our nearest star. It is a great ball of very hot gases swirling in space. All the time it pours out heat and light as atoms

of hydrogen gas join together inside it to form atoms of another gas – helium. Life on Earth depends on this heat and light. Without it, the Earth would be a dark, cold, dead lump of rock. All living things need warmth, and plants need sunlight to make food.

The Sun is very much like many other stars in the sky. It appears bigger and hotter only because it is much nearer than the other stars. But compared with the Earth, the Sun is very big indeed. You could get more than a million Earths inside the Sun. The Earth is part of the Sun's family, or solar system. It is one of nine planets circling around the Sun.

See also PLANET; STAR.

Mute swan

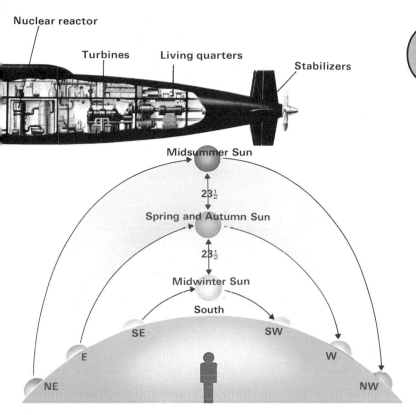

Nuclear reactor

Turbines   Living quarters

Stabilizers

Midsummer Sun

$23\frac{1}{2}$

Spring and Autumn Sun

$23\frac{1}{2}$

Midwinter Sun

South

SE   SW

E   W

NE   NW

SWAN

People admire these birds for their grace and beauty. Most kinds are white, but there are black swans in Australia. Swans live on rivers and lakes, and feed on plants and small water animals. They nest by the water. Young swans are called cygnets.

SWITZERLAND

This small land-locked country is in central Europe. It borders on Germany, Italy, France, Liechtenstein and Austria.

Between the spectacular snow-

▲ **The Sun's** daily path across the sky changes at different times of the year. This is because our Earth orbits the Sun at an angle.

capped Alps in south-eastern Switzerland and the Jura Mountains in the north-west is the Swiss Plateau. On this plain are Switzerland's most important towns and large industries. Here, too, most of the country's crops are grown.

Swiss factories produce goods such as machinery, watches and chemicals. Tourism is also a major industry. See also page 64.

TAX

The government needs money to run the country. It gets this money mainly from the taxes we pay. Taxes pay for the roads, schools, hospitals and many other services a country needs.

There are several kinds of taxes. Most people pay tax on their income – the money they earn. Income tax is a *direct tax*. *Indirect* taxes are taxes on goods and services. A value added tax (VAT) is paid on goods we buy. Customs duties are paid when goods enter the country. Excise duties are put on goods such as tobacco and alcohol. Rates are *local* taxes paid by householders to the local councils.

TEA

Tea is made by pouring boiling water on to tea leaves. The leaves come from tea bushes, which are grown mainly in India, Sri Lanka and China. Tea first came to Europe from China in the 1600s. At first it was brewed and stored in barrels, like beer.

TEETH

Teeth cut and chew food into pieces small enough to be swal-

▲ **Tea pickers** on a plantation in Asia.

lowed. The kinds of teeth an animal has depends on the kind of food it eats.

Beasts of prey, such as wolves and lions, have long sharp teeth. They use them to kill their prey and to tear the meat. Rodents, such as squirrels, have gnawing teeth. Grazing animals, such as cattle, have flat grinding teeth.

Human beings have sharp cutting teeth *and* flat grinding teeth. This is because we eat both meat and plant food.

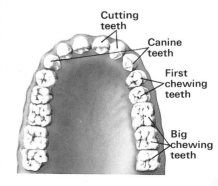

208

TELEPHONE

The first telephone calls could only be sent through wires. Now a telephone call may travel by wire, or by radio, sometimes bounced off satellites. When you dial a number, the telephone sends out electrical pulses. They go to an exchange, which automatically connects you to the number you dialled.

When you talk, a microphone changes your voice into electrical signals. These travel down the wires to the earpiece of the person you are talking to. There they are changed back into the sound of your voice.

TELESCOPE

A telescope is an instrument that makes distant objects appear nearer and larger.

The simplest type, a refracting telescope, consists of a tube containing two lenses which bend the light rays from the distant object and make it appear nearer.

THE TELEPHONE HANDSET

T

Electro-magnet

Earpiece

Mouthpiece

Diaphragm

Carbon granules

▼ **A refracting** telescope. The small finder helps to locate objects.

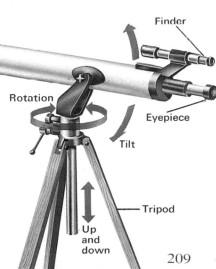

Finder

Rotation

Eyepiece

Tilt

Tripod

Up and down

Most astronomers, however, use reflecting telescopes, which have a mirror to collect and bend the light. They are bigger and clearer than refracting telescopes.

As well as light telescopes, astronomers use radio telescopes: large metal dishes which gather radio waves sent out by heavenly bodies.

209

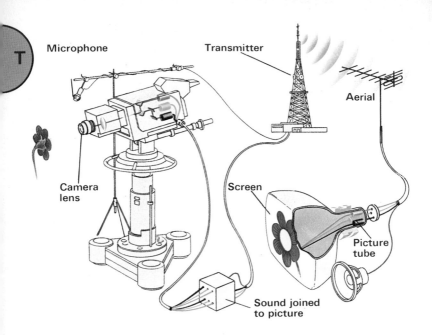

Microphone   Transmitter

Aerial

Camera lens

Screen

Picture tube

Sound joined to picture

TELEVISION

'Television' means 'pictures from a distance'. Television can show us live pictures of events on the other side of the world.

Two important pieces of television equipment are the *camera* and the *receiver*. The camera records an image of the scene it views on an electrically charged plate. A beam of electrons then sweeps back and forth across this plate. The result is electric signals which represent the brightness in different parts of the scene. These signals are combined with a radio wave and sent out by a transmitter.

The aerial of the television set picks up the wave. Circuits in the set separate the signal from the wave. These signals then go to

the picture tube where a 'gun' fires a beam of electrons at the screen causing a spot of light. The television signals alter the strength of the beam and thereby the brightness of the spot. They also make the beam sweep back and forth in a series of lines of spots of varying brightness. The lines are very close together, and our eyes see them as a complete picture.

TENNIS

When we use the word tennis we are usually referring to the game of lawn tennis. This game is played on hard or grass courts. Two people play in a singles match; four people in a doubles match. Tennis today is a form of an old French game.

THEATRE

The first theatres were in ancient Greece. People sat in the open air on a hillside, while below actors and dancers performed on a space called the orchestra. Behind the actors was a changing room called the skene. This later became a stage, and it gives us the modern words 'scenery' and 'scene'.

England's first real theatres were built in the 1500s. Each had a jutting stage almost surrounded by the audience. Rich people sat under cover. Poor spectators stood in the 'pit', and got wet if it rained. But soon all theatres had roofs. Complicated scenery and stage machinery began to be used. And to hide the workings from the audience, a 'picture frame' was put round the stage. The audience now only sat in front of it. Some modern theatres have gone back to the old idea.

See also PLAY.

▼ A tropical thunderstorm near Darwin, Australia.

THERMOMETER

A thermometer measures temperature – how hot it is. Most thermometers consist of a thin tube with a bulb of liquid. When liquids are heated, they expand, or grow bigger. So when the liquid in the bulb becomes hotter, it rises up the tube. The liquid used is generally mercury or coloured alcohol.

Every thermometer has a scale marked on it. The most common scale is the Celsius, or centigrade scale. On this scale, the freezing point of water is 0 degrees, and the boiling point 100 degrees.

THUNDERSTORM

About 44,000 thunderstorms occur each day, mainly in the tropics. Lightning may flash in sheets, in balls or in forked streaks. The thunder is produced by the sudden expansion of air that has been heated by the lightning flash. Thunder is heard after a flash because light travels faster than sound.

See also LIGHTNING.

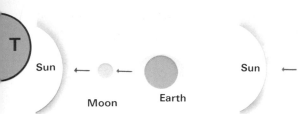

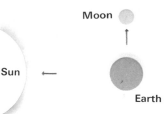

SPRING TIDE

NEAP TIDE

▲ **The position** of the Sun, Moon and Earth at Spring and Neap tides.

TIDES

Tides are caused by the Moon and the Sun pulling the world's oceans towards them. This is the result of gravity. Because the Moon is closer to Earth than the Sun is, its pull is stronger.

There are roughly two high tides and two low tides every 24 hours. When the Moon and Sun are on the same side of the Earth, their combined pull produces the biggest tides, called *spring tides*. When the Moon and Sun are pulling at right angles to each other, the smallest tides, called *neap tides*, occur.

TIGER

The tiger is the largest of the big cats. Its home is Asia. Most tigers live in hot forests. But the largest come from cold Siberia.

Tigers hunt alone and at night. They prey on deer, wild cattle and pigs. Only an old or sick tiger will attack people. The tiger's stripes camouflage it in long grass. Unlike other cats, tigers often bathe to keep cool.

TIME

The day is a natural unit of time. It is the time the Earth takes to spin round once in space. Our other main natural unit of time is the year – the time it takes the Earth to travel once round the Sun. There are $365\frac{1}{4}$ days in a year.

The Moon circles the Earth about every 27 days. This gives us another unit of time – the month. Our calendar has 12 months each year.

We measure time, or rather the passage of time, with clocks and

▼ **The tiger** is the largest of the big cats.

watches. They help us split each day into 24 hours; each hour into 60 minutes; and each minute into 60 seconds. Day, hour, minute and second are units of time. We can say what time it is in two ways – by a 12-hour clock or a 24-hour clock.

See also CALENDAR; CLOCKS AND WATCHES.

TIN
Tin is a common but very important metal. It resists corrosion (being eaten away) by acids and is often used for protective coatings, such as on the inside of tins of food. Its most important use is in alloys like bronze and brass.

TOBACCO
Tobacco is made from the dried leaves of the tobacco plant. It originally grew wild in America. The Spaniards brought tobacco to Europe in the 1500s, and today tobacco is grown in Asia, Africa and Europe as well as America.

Tobacco leaf can be made into pipe, cigar or cigarette tobacco, or snuff. Smoking is a harmful habit. It is especially bad for the lungs and heart.

TORTOISE AND TURTLE
Unlike other reptiles, tortoises and turtles have hard shells to protect their bodies.

Tortoises are land animals. They live in warm countries and eat plant food. A tortoise cannot run away from an enemy. Instead, it tucks its head and legs into its shell. Some tortoises can live to be much more than a hundred years old – older than any other animals.

▼ **Cigars** must be stored at special temperatures.

213

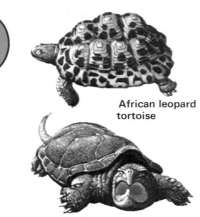

African leopard tortoise

Snapping turtle

Turtles live in the sea. They have flatter shells than tortoises, and use their legs as paddles for swimming. On land they are very clumsy.

See also REPTILE.

TOUCAN

These brightly coloured birds live in the tropical forests of South and Central America. They have harsh ugly cries and eat almost anything. Their beaks are enormous – sometimes 16 centimetres long – but they are almost as light as sponge rubber.

TRADE UNION

Trade unions are organizations or associations of workers. By joining together in a union, workers are better able to negotiate, or bargain, with their employers for higher wages or better working conditions.

Trade unions began during the Industrial Revolution in the 1700s. Many workers were badly paid, and their work was often unhealthy or dangerous. The trade unions had a long struggle to improve conditions.

TRANSISTOR

A transistor is a small electronic device used to *amplify* or to strengthen signals in electronic equipment such as radios, computers and satellites. It is made from crystals of material such as germanium or silicon.

Transistors were invented in 1948. A large number of them can be put in a silicon chip a few millimetres square.

See also SILICON CHIP.

TREE

Trees are the largest of all plants. The world's biggest tree is the Californian redwood which can reach a height of over 100 metres. Trees grow a little each year. The tips of their branches grow longer, and a ring of tissue in the main trunk and the older branches produces more cells to make them thicker.

Evergreen trees keep their leaves all year round. Conifers, such as spruce, pine and fir, are evergreens. They grow in colder climates. Their leaves are thin and hard, and look like needles. Conifers do not have flowers; instead, they have winged seeds hidden inside cones.

Many tropical trees are also evergreens. But they have broad leaves, and flowers. Broadleaved trees grow in cool countries too.

Beech   Common oak   Aspen   Yew

Elm   Bird cherry   Larch   Sweet chestnut

Scots pine   Wych elm   Alder   Field maple

Black poplar   Sycamore   Ash   Walnut

Those that shed their leaves in autumn are called *deciduous*.

TSUNAMI

When an earthquake occurs on the ocean floor it produces great waves called tsunamis. They travel long distances at speeds of up to 800 kilometres per hour. In the open ocean they may be only a metre or so high, but when they run into shallow water and slow down they rise rapidly to heights of from 10 to 30 metres.

ULTRA-VIOLET RAYS

Light from the Sun can be split by a prism into a *spectrum* of colour. Red is at one end of the spectrum, violet at the other. Ultra-violet rays are found beyond the violet end of the spectrum.

These rays are very useful and important, although we cannot see them. They produce vitamin D in our bodies, which is necessary for growing bones. Ultra-violet rays can be used to kill bacteria.

USSR

When people talk about 'Russia' they usually mean the 'Union of Soviet Socialist Republics', for this is the country's full name. Fifteen republics make up the USSR, the largest country in the world, 22,402,200 square kilometres, stretching from Europe right across Asia to the Pacific Ocean.

There are many different regions in such a huge land, and many different climates. The rugged Ural Mountains separate Europe from Asia. Beyond are wide treeless plains – the steppes. In each region there are different

▲ **St Basil's Cathedral** stands Moscow, the capital of the USSR.

plants and animals. The north has a cold Arctic climate. But in the warm south fruit, tea and even palm trees grow. In the cool *taiga* zone the forests provide huge amounts of timber, while on the fertile steppes wheat and other crops are grown.

Farming is important and so are fishing, the fur trade and mining. There are rich deposits of minerals, including coal, oil, iron ore, manganese and gold. All farms, factories, mines and shops are run by the government.

Until 1917 Russia was an empire. Then in 1917 there was a revolution. The Tsar, Nicholas II, was overthrown, and Vladimir Lenin set up a Communist government. Today the USSR rivals the USA as the richest and strongest country in the world.

See also page 64.

216

UNITED KINGDOM

England, Scotland, Wales and Northern Ireland together make up the United Kingdom of Great Britain and Northern Ireland. The head of state is the Queen, but parliament makes the laws, and the government is led by the prime minister.

The climate is mild, with plenty of rainfall. In this rather crowded country, most people live in towns. Farming is important, but the farmers cannot produce enough, so food has to be imported.

There is coal underground, and natural gas and oil offshore beneath the sea. Together these fuels help to provide power for the nation's many industries. Heavy industries are mainly in northern England, South Wales and Scotland. Many people live in and around London, the capital and business centre.

England was conquered by the Romans and later by the Normans. In the 1200s the English conquered Wales. From 1603 England and Scotland had the same king; and from 1707 they shared a single parliament. Ireland joined the union in 1801, but southern Ireland broke away in 1921 and later became a republic. See also page 64.

UNITED NATIONS

In the present century there have been two terrible world wars. The United Nations was set up in 1945 to try and prevent wars.

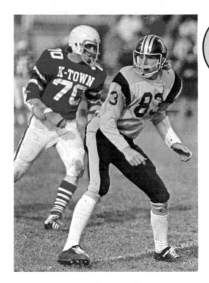

▲ **American footballers** are protected by helmets and pads.

The UN tries to settle quarrels between countries peacefully. It helps refugees and children, and sends experts to fight hunger, disease and ignorance in poor countries. The headquarters of the UN are in New York. Here the General Assembly and the Security Council meet to discuss world problems.

UNITED STATES OF AMERICA

Fifty states make up the United States of America – the USA. This huge country consists of the middle part of North America, Alaska in the far north and Hawaii in the Pacific Ocean.

The climate varies from region to region. Some areas are hot in summer and cold in winter, but

217

the south and west coasts have mild winters. Most regions get good rainfall.

The United States has very great natural resources. Its farmland is fertile. Huge crops of wheat are grown on the prairies, and maize (corn), tobacco, cotton, fruit and vegetables are also grown. From the forests comes timber, while underground are valuable minerals, including coal, oil, natural gas, iron, gold, copper and uranium. Many rivers and lakes have been dammed to produce electricity.

More than half the people live in towns and cities, for the United States is the greatest industrial country in the world. Its factories make aircraft, cars, computers, machines, and many other kinds of goods.

The first Americans were the Indians, who lived by farming and hunting. But after Columbus' discovery of the 'New World', Europeans began settling in America. Beginning in the 1600s, the British set up thirteen colonies on the east coast. But the colonists wanted to govern themselves, and in 1776 they broke away from Britain and became an independent republic, the United States of America, with George Washington as the first President.

The republic grew into a union of fifty states. Many poor people from European countries came to the United States. Industry developed so quickly that the Americans soon enjoyed a higher standard of living than any other people in the world.

See also page 65.

▼ **The Big Bang**. Most people now think the Universe began with a huge explosion. These pictures show how the galaxies might have formed, gradually moving apart away from the explosion and each other.

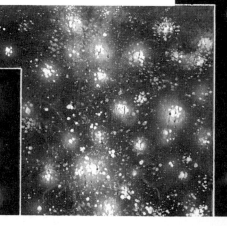

UNIVERSE

When we talk of the Universe, we mean everything that exists. This includes the air, the sea, the Earth, the other planets, the Moon, the stars and space.

Years ago people thought that the Earth was the centre of the Universe. They thought that all the other heavenly bodies circled around it. About 500 years ago people began to realize that the Earth was not the centre.

Now we know that the Earth is only a tiny speck in the Universe. It belongs to the Sun's family of stars called the Galaxy. The Galaxy belongs to a family of galaxies. And there are millions of such families in the Universe.

But most of the Universe is just empty space.

URANIUM

This element is a rare whitish metal. It is radioactive, that is it gives off rays which cannot be seen but which will darken film.

Although it was discovered in 1789, uranium had very few uses until 1940. Then a method of obtaining energy from it was discovered. When uranium is bombarded with neutrons its atoms become unstable. They split and give off energy. This splitting process is called fission. Uranium is used for nuclear power and in atomic bombs.

See also NUCLEAR POWER.

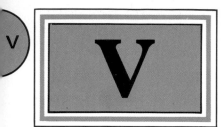

VEGETABLE

Many of the plants we eat are called 'vegetables'. Vegetables are good food, supplying energy or body-building substances.

Various parts of vegetables are eaten. Potatoes are root vegetables, spinach is a leaf, brussel sprouts are leaf buds and broccoli is a flower. Some fruits and seeds are eaten as vegetables. Tomatoes and cucumbers are fruits; peas and beans are seeds.

VICTORIA (1819–1901)

Queen Victoria reigned for 64 years, longer than any other British monarch. She became Queen when she was only 18. Victoria loved her husband, Prince Albert, very dearly. After he died in 1861, she spent the rest of her life in mourning. During her reign, Britain grew to be a mighty industrial nation, ruling a huge empire.

VIKING

In the 8th century fierce Vikings from Scandinavia began raiding the coasts of western Europe. They burned villages, robbed churches, stole cattle and carried off slaves. People were terrified of them, especially as Vikings often fought like madmen, as if eager to die in battle.

But the Vikings were not just pirates and robbers. They were also farmers and traders. Their craftsmen were highly skilled in using iron, gold and silver.

In their long ships (wooden boats with oars and square sails) they crossed the Atlantic Ocean to settle in Iceland and Greenland. They probably reached America around AD 1000. The Vikings also settled in Ireland, France, Russia and England.

VITAMIN

Vitamins are chemicals our bodies need for healthy growth. We get vitamins from food. From lettuce, carrots, butter and eggs comes *Vitamin A*. It helps us grow. There are several kinds of *Vitamin B*. We eat them in cereals, milk, meat, vegetables and fruit. *Vitamin C* is found in fruit. *Vitamin D* is important to babies. It prevents a bone disease called rickets. Egg yolks and liver are rich in vitamin D. Sunlight has the same effect. Other vitamins are known as *E* and *K*. The body only uses vitamins in tiny quantities. A good varied diet gives it all the vitamins it needs.

VOLCANO

Volcanoes occur where the Earth's crust is being squeezed or stretched as new mountains are formed. The enormous pressures melt the solid rock to liquid magma. When the pressures become too great, gases and hot liquid rock, called *lava*, may burst through the centre of a volcano and out of a pit or crater at the top.

Volcanoes are usually cone-shaped with a crater at the top. Active volcanoes erupt for short periods and then remain dormant for long periods. If the lava remains bubbling in a lava lake, eruptions are just overflows. If, however, the lava solidifies, the next eruption will explode.

▼ **Inside a volcano.** Hot lava and melted rock spout up from the central vent. The mountain is made from layers of cold ash and lava.

WAR

People have always found it difficult to live in peace together. From prehistoric times envy and greed have made one tribe attack another, in order to steal its land or animals. Later great empires were founded by conquering armies.

'In ancient Greece and Rome soldiers were armed with swords, spears, slings and bows and arrows. Foot soldiers, or infantry, made up the largest part of an army. The Roman armies were so well trained that for hundreds of years they were unbeatable.

Horsemen, or cavalry, played an important part in wars throughout the Middle Ages. Knights in armour, armed with lances, swords and clubs, battered their way through enemy ranks. But if a skilled archer killed his horse, the clumsy knight was helpless on foot.

Gunpowder came into use in the 1300s. From then on wars were fought increasingly with guns. But it took many years before soldiers had guns light enough to carry easily.

By 1914 guns were so powerful that soldiers had to dig trenches for protection. During World War I whole armies were bogged down in trenches, unable to move more than a few kilometres. and millions of soldiers were killed. The tank, first used in 1916, was a powerful new

▼ **Civilians** are often the victims in today's wars fought with efficient tanks and missiles.

weapon. Even more deadly was the aeroplane. For the first time civilians were attacked in their homes by bombs dropped from fighter planes in the air.

World War II was fought in Europe, Africa and Asia. Most of the world's leading nations took part. It was a war of rapid movement. Submarines sank many ships with their torpedoes. The war against Japan ended with the dropping of the first atomic bombs on the cities of Hiroshima and Nagasaki. These nuclear weapons are the most terrible ever known in warfare.

See also CIVIL WAR.

MAJOR WARS

Some of the most important wars fought since the Fall of the Roman Empire in AD 476.

1337–1453	Hundred Years' War
1455–1485	Wars of the Roses
1618–1648	Thirty Years' War
1642–1651	English Civil War
1701 1713	War of Spanish Succession
1740–1748	War of Austrian Succession
1756–1763	Seven Years' War
1775–1783	American War of Independence
1792–1815	Napoleonic Wars
1812–1814	War of 1812
1854–1856	Crimean War
1861–1865	American Civil War
1870–1871	Franco-Prussian War
1899–1902	Boer War (South Africa)
1914–1918	World War I
1936–1939	Spanish Civil War
1939–1945	World War II
1957–1975	Vietnam War
1973	Yom Kippur War
1980	Iran-Iraq War

WASHINGTON, George
(1732–99)

George Washington, the first President of the USA was a farmer from Virginia. When the American colonists fought the British in the War of Independence from 1775 to 1783, Washington became general of their army. In 1789 he became President, although he did not consider himself fit for such an important task.

WASP

Wasps are related to ants and bees. They are hunting insects, and many wasps will sting if annoyed.

Social wasps live in colonies. Inside the nest, the queen lays eggs, while workers care for the eggs and larvae. Adult wasps eat nectar. But the larvae are fed on insects and caterpillars. In the autumn all the wasps die, except for the young queens. They hibernate, and start new nests in the spring. Solitary wasps live alone and build small nests.

▼ **A potter wasp** moulds mud into a pot-shaped nest.

223

Water shapes the land carving out canyons and forming lakes. It is essential for crops to grow, for people to drink, and for many factory processes. The power of falling water can also be used to generate electricity.

Glacier

Waterfall

Reservoir which supplies water to factories and homes

A hydro-electric power station where the power of falling water is used to make electricity

Canyon

River

Lake

WATER

Water is the most precious liquid on Earth, for without it, nothing can live.

Water is the only mineral that is liquid. It is made up of the chemical elements hydrogen and oxygen. Its molecules contain two atoms of hydrogen (H) to one atom of oxygen (O). We write this as the chemical formula H_2O.

Water plays an important part in our weather. The Sun warms the Earth's water changing some of it into vapour. The vapour rises and, as it does so, condenses and falls back to the ground as rain or snow. This continuous process is called the water cycle.

Water also shapes the Earth. Rain, ocean waves and rivers weather and erode the land. Glaciers gouge paths through rocks and soil.

Water power helps people. Great dams can harness the power of water to make electricity. We call this form of power hydro-electricity.

See also ENERGY; GLACIER; ICE; LAKE; RAIN; RIVER; OCEANS.

WATERFALL

A waterfall is caused by water wearing away rock at different speeds. If a river flows over a join between hard rock and soft rock, it wears away the soft rock more quickly and makes a deep 'step'. Some waterfalls are quite small, but in some places wide rivers fall over huge cliffs. The most famous waterfalls are Niagara, between Canada and the United States and the Victoria Falls in Africa. The highest is Angel Falls in Venezuela.

WATT, James (1736–1819)

Watt was a Scottish engineer who invented a more efficient steam engine than any before. He devised a condenser and several methods of changing the motion of a piston into the rotating motion of a wheel.

WEST INDIES

The islands known as the West Indies lie between the Caribbean Sea and the Atlantic Ocean. The many islands are divided into more than 20 countries. The largest are Cuba, Jamaica, Haiti and the Dominican Republic.

Most of the islands have a tropical climate and people grow sugar, tobacco, cocoa, coffee, coconuts, bananas and other fruits. There is not much industry but iron ore, bauxite and asphalt are mined. Many islands have a busy tourist industry.

The West Indies were discovered in 1492 by Christopher Columbus. Spain conquered the islands in the 1500s and later the British, French and Dutch set up colonies there. African slaves were brought to work on plantations. Today most islands run their own affairs. Most West Indians speak English, French or Spanish. See also page 65.

WHALE

Although whales spend all their lives in the sea, they are mammals, not fish. Whales are warm-blooded. They have skin, not scales. The females give birth to live young and feed them on milk. Although a whale can dive to great depths, loading its blood with enough oxygen to last for up to 45 minutes, it must surface to breathe. Whales swim by beating their tails up and down.

There are two families of whales: toothed whales, and whalebone or baleen whales.

WHEEL

The wheel is one of the most important inventions. A great deal of human and animal energy is saved through using it.

No one knows when the wheel was invented. Its first use was probably as a potter's wheel in Mesopotamia about 5000 years ago. Wheels were next used on carts. These wheels were solid, made by cutting slices off large tree trunks.

Without wheels, advanced transport systems would not be possible. They are essential to most machines and engines.

WILLIAM THE CONQUEROR (*c.*1027–1087)

In 1066 William, Duke of Normandy, landed with his army in Sussex and defeated and killed King Harold. He was crowned William I, the first Norman king of England.

William was an efficient administrator. He caused a great survey of the land to be made. It is known as the Domesday Book. William's descendants ruled England for many years after his death.

WIND

Wind is the movement of air over the Earth's surface. The chief cause of wind is the unequal heating of the Earth's surface. At the Equator, which gets most heat from the Sun, air becomes warm and rises. At the Poles, which are the coldest places, cold air sinks. As the warm air rises, cool air moves in to take its place. Changing temperatures over the sea and land also affect the pattern of the winds.

Winds are named after the direction from which they come; so a north wind blows from the north, and so on.

◀ **Blue Whales** have baleen instead of teeth. The rows of bony plates filter water and trap lots of tiny prawn-like animals.

▼ **An egg-beater** windmill, Albuquerque, USA.

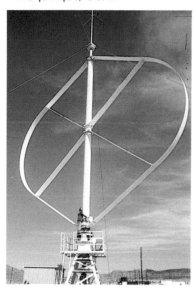

WINDMILL

Windmills are used to grind corn, pump water and generate electricity. Their source of power is the wind. Sails or blades are fixed to a shaft. The shaft is connected to the machinery to be driven. As other forms of energy become expensive, windmills may again become popular. A light steel type has been devised in the USA for use on farms.

WITCH

A witch is a person who is supposed to have made a pact with the Devil. She (or he) agrees to do the Devil's work and in return is given magic powers.

Today, few people believe in witches but at one time everyone did. Witches were persecuted all over western Europe from the 15th to the 19th century. During this time at least 200,000 men and women were killed because they were thought to be witches.

There have been many famous witches in fact and fiction. Joan of Arc was burned as a witch in 1431. The Witch of Endor is mentioned in the Bible and Medea is a witch in Greek myth.

WOLF

Wolves belong to the dog family. They are strong, intelligent animals and often hunt together in packs. They will chase a deer for many hours until the prey is exhausted. Wolves also eat smaller animals, and will attack cattle and sheep. The grey timber wolf of North America, Europe and Asia is the largest wolf. All kinds are now quite rare.

▼ **The European** timber wolf lives in northern forests.

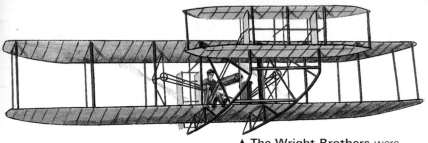

WOOD

Wood is used in building, in making furniture and is burned as fuel. Cut wood is called timber. The timber we get from coniferous trees, such as pine, is called softwood. The timber we get from deciduous trees, such as oak, is called hardwood. Softwoods are used mainly in building construction, hardwoods for furniture.

Wood is also made into paper, textile fibres, plastics, explosives and several other chemicals. The main chemical substance in wood is cellulose.

▲ **The Wright Brothers** were the first to build and successfully fly an aeroplane.

WOOL

Wool is the fine hair obtained from the fleece of sheep. It is one of the oldest fibres used for making clothes and other textiles. Wool fibres are naturally crinkled which helps woollen garments keep their shape. Each fibre is covered with tiny overlapping scales so that the fibres lock together when they are spun into yarn. A Merino ram can give up to 12 kilogrammes of wool.

▼ **Felling soft-wood** trees in the USA.

WORM

Worms are animals with soft bodies. Some live underground or in water, others as parasites inside plants or other animals.

There are about 20,000 different kinds of worms. One group includes *flatworms* which have flat, ribbon or leaf-shaped bodies. The harmful parasites, the tapeworm and the liver fluke are flatworms. Threadworms, roundworms and hookworms are found in another group. Many of these are also parasites. *Segmented worms* are not harmful. Their bodies are made up of segments or rings. They include ragworms, lugworms and the earthworm.

See also PARASITE.

Ribbonworm

WRIGHT, Orville (1871–1948) and Wilber (1867–1912)

These two American brothers made the first motor-powered, heavier-than-air flight in 1903.

They taught themselves about flight by making and flying kites and gliders. By 1903 they were ready to attach a four-cylinder, 13-horse-power engine to a biplane glider. On December 17th, Orville took off, rose to a height of nearly 3 metres and flew over 35 metres. The flight took 59 seconds.

X-RAY

X-rays are invisible waves of energy like light waves. They can pass through and into most materials. They pass through flesh, for example. In hospitals doctors take X-ray photographs to look inside the body. A patient stands in front of a photographic film and X-rays are passed through him. When the film is developed, the patient's bones show up. This is because the bones block some of the rays and cast a shadow on the film. The doctors can see if any of the bones are broken. Some new X-ray machines can photograph body organs as well.

X-rays were discovered by the German scientist Wilhelm Röntgen in 1895.

▼ **This X-ray** shows the hand of a four-year-old boy.

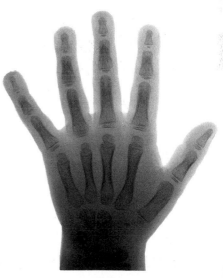

YAK

Yaks live in the cold, high mountains of central Asia. Yaks are among the largest wild cattle, yet they climb as nimbly as goats. The yak can live on poor pasture and is very useful to the people of the Himalayas. It gives milk, butter and meat, its skin is made into leather, and its long hair is woven into cloth.

YUGOSLAVIA

The great river Danube flows through the north of this mountainous country in south-eastern Europe. Farmers here grow wheat, barley, olives and grapes. Different groups live in the country, such as the Slavs and Croats, and each group has its own language. Belgrade is the capital. See also page 64.

ZAIRE

This hot rainy country is in central Africa. The River Zaire, once called the Congo, runs right through the rain forest. Cobalt, copper and diamonds are mined in Zaire but most of the people work on farms. See also page 64.

ZAMBIA

Zambia is a land-locked country in Southern Africa. Copper mining is very important – nearly a quarter of all the copper in the world comes from Zambia.

The Zambezi river, which Zambia shares with Zimbabwe, has been dammed to form Lake Kariba. See also page 64.

ZIMBABWE

Most people in this country are farmers. They grow food crops and crops like sugar cane, tobacco and fruit to sell to other countries.

For a long time Zimbabwe was a British colony called Rhodesia. It became the republic of Zimbabwe in 1980. See also page 64.

◀ **The yak's** shaggy coat keeps it warm in its mountain home.

ZOO

A zoo is a place where wild animals are kept in captivity. People enjoy going to zoos to see animals from other countries. But more important, zoos help to save rare animals from becoming extinct. Zoos around the world exchange animals and try to breed them.

In the past, kings collected wild animals in zoos. The first public zoos began in the 19th century. Often the cages were too small for the animals and the bars made it hard for people to see them properly.

Today zoos have enclosures in which the animals feel more at home. Ditches, moats and glass keep the animals and visitors apart. Birds fly about inside large aviaries. Mountain goats climb artificial hills, while penguins, polar bears, seals and even elephants have pools to splash in. In special darkened builings, people can see animals which are normally active only at night.

ZOOLOGY

This is the science that deals with the study of animals. Zoologists find out about animals' bodies, their growth patterns and habits. About a million different species, or kinds, of animals have been described by zoologists and sorted into groups.

The study of zoology helps us to understand animals, to control animal pests and diseases, and to improve the quality of farm animals.

▼ Children feed elephants at a zoo.

231

Index

ACKNOWLEDGEMENTS

Photographs: Alabama Bureau of Publicity 126; Ames Europe Ltd 143 *top;* Australian News & Information Bureau 141; Associated Press 101; Bodleian Library, Oxford cover *top right;* J. Allan Cash 98; Ceylon Tea Centre 208; Michael Chinery 107; J. E. Clapham 103 *top right;* Dave Collins 39, 42, Geological Museum 103 *top left;* Giraudon 145; Michael Holford 122 *bottom;* Iraq Cultural Institute cover *top centre;* Iraq Tourist 150; Italian Institute 144; Italian Tourist 55; Japan Tourist 54; Kunst historiches Museum, Austria 165; Mansell Collection 11, 70 *top;* Mauritshuis, The Hague 182; Met Office 211; Metropolitan Police 91; Pat Morris 97, 163; NASA 100, 143 *bottom;* Dave Nash 198; NHPA 70 *bottom;* National Portrait Gallery 130; Nature Photographs 4, 34, 167, 184; New Zealand House 104; Novosti 139 *top;* Pitti Gallery, Florence 165 *top left;* Royal National Institute for the Blind 37; Sandia Laboratories 227; SATOUR cover *centre right,* 106; Science Museum 168; Shell UK Ltd 161; Siemens Ltd 142; Adrian Sington 160; Frank Spooner Pictures 96, 222; Tampa Chamber of Commerce 213; Tate Gallery 165 *top right,* 190; U.S. Environmental Protection Agency 173; U.S. Naval Observatory 204; Westland Helicopters 111; D & J Wright 105; Zefa UK Ltd cover *bottom, centre left,* 15, 27, 45, 52, 53, 77, 78, 110, 120, 122 *top,* 183, 216, 230, 231.

Picture Research: Penny Warn